BRITISH AUTHORS

Introductory Critical Studies

General Editor: ROBIN MAYHEAD

E. M. FORSTER

D1529635

In this series

Understanding Literature by ROBIN MAYHEAD

John Keats by ROBIN MAYHEAD

William Wordsworth by GEOFFREY DURRANT

George Eliot by R. T. JONES

Jane Austen by YASMINE GOONERATNE

William Blake by D. G. GILLHAM

Walter Scott by ROBIN MAYHEAD

Alexander Pope by YASMINE GOONERATNE

E. M. FORSTER

The endless journey

BY

JOHN SAYRE MARTIN

Associate Professor of English
University of Calgary, Alberta

CAMBRIDGE UNIVERSITY PRESS

CAMBRIDGE

LONDON · NEW YORK · MELBOURNE

Published by the Syndics of the Cambridge University Press
The Pitt Building, Trumpington Street, Cambridge CB2 1RP
Bentley House, 200 Euston Road, London NW1 2DB
32 East 57th Street, New York, NY 10022, USA
296 Beaconsfield Parade, Middle Park, Melbourne 3206, Australia

Library of Congress catalogue card number: 76-4755

ISBN 0 521 21272 3 hard covers
ISBN 0 521 29082 1 paperback

First published 1976

Printed in Great Britain
at the
University Printing House, Cambridge
(Euan Phillips, University Printer)

General Preface

This study of E. M. Forster is the eighth in a series of short introductory critical studies of the more important British authors. The aim of the series is to go straight to the authors' works; to discuss them directly with a maximum of attention to concrete detail; to say what they are and what they do, and to indicate a valuation. The general critical attitude implied in the series is set out at some length in my *Understanding Literature*. Great literature is taken to be to a large extent self-explanatory to the reader who will attend carefully enough to what it says. 'Background' study, whether biographical or historical, is not the concern of the series.

It is hoped that this approach will suit a number of kinds of reader, in particular the general reader who would like an introduction which talks about the works themselves; and the student who would like a general critical study as a starting point, intending to go on to read more specialized works later. Since 'background' is not erected as an insuperable obstacle, readers in other English-speaking countries, countries where English is a second language, or even those for whom English is a foreign language, should find the books helpful. In Britain and the Commonwealth, students and teachers in universities and in the higher forms of secondary schools will find that the authors chosen for treatment are those most often prescribed for study in public and university examinations.

The series could be described as an attempt to make available to a wide public the results of the literary criticism of the last thirty years, and especially the methods associated with Cambridge. If the result is an increase in the reading, with enjoyment and understanding, of the great works of English literature, the books will have fulfilled their wider purpose.

ROBIN MAYHEAD

To Concie

Contents

Acknowledgements   *page* viii

Introduction   1

1 *Where Angels Fear to Tread*   13

2 *The Longest Journey*   26

3 The Short Stories   48

4 *A Room with a View*   89

5 *Howards End*   109

6 *Maurice*   128

7 *A Passage to India*   143

  Conclusion   164

Acknowledgements

For help in preparing this book, I should like to thank the following individuals: Professor Robert J. Kiely of Harvard University and Mr Oliver Stallybrass for constructively criticizing parts of the manuscript; The Provost and Scholars of King's College, Cambridge for kindly allowing me to consult and reproduce some of the unpublished Forster material in their Library; and Miss Elizabeth Ellem of the King's College Library for her time and help. I am grateful to Forster's friend William Roerick of Tyringham, Massachusetts, and that pioneer critic of Forster's writing, the late Lionel Trilling, for the opportunity of discussing Forster with them. Finally, I should like to thank the Canada Council for supporting my research with a grant.

Needless to say, for any shortcomings that the book may have I alone am responsible.

Introduction

I

Despite widespread agreement that E. M. Forster is one of the most important English novelists of the present century, he is a writer who has puzzled, and perhaps continues to puzzle, discerning readers and critics. The sheer number of books and articles that have appeared on his work over the past twenty years is testimony to the fact that Forster's most interesting qualities do not always lie close to the surface. In 1927, I. A. Richards declared Forster to be 'the most puzzling figure in contemporary English letters'. He seems tacitly to assume, according to Richards, that the reader shares his rather 'unusual outlook on life', an assumption that can lead to some 'lamentable misunderstandings'.[1] Virginia Woolf also found something 'baffling and evasive' in the very nature of Forster's gifts. For her, his combination of 'poetry' and realism, of mysticism and fact, failed to cohere into the single vision that marks the great novelist.[2] Lionel Trilling, in his pioneer study of Forster, saw him as a moral realist, but an evasive one. 'The plot', he writes, 'speaks of clear certainties, the manner resolutely insists that nothing can be quite so simple. "Wash ye, make yourselves clean," says the plot, and the manner murmurs, "if you can find the soap."'[3] According to Philip Gardner, one of the most common adjectives that reviewers and critics have applied to Forster's fiction is 'elusive'.[4]

In one sense Forster's elusiveness is a quality of his style, which is both personal and evasive. Like many Victorian

---

[1] I. A. Richards, 'A Passage to Forster: Reflections on a Novelist', reprinted in *Forster, A Collection of Critical Essays*, ed. Malcolm Bradbury, pp. 15–20. Englewood Cliffs, N.J., 1966.

[2] Virginia Woolf, 'The Novels of E. M. Forster', in *Collected Essays*, vol. 1, pp. 342–51. London, 1966.

[3] Lionel Trilling, *E. M. Forster*, p. 12. Norfolk, Conn., 1943.

[4] Philip Gardner, *E. M. Forster, The Critical Heritage*, p. 12. London, 1973.

I

novelists, he often obtrusively comments upon his characters and incidents and indulges in moral generalizations. But he is just as likely to mask his opinion with a qualifying 'perhaps' or a form of rhetorical ventriloquism in which he suddenly projects a view, apparently his, upon one or more of his characters. Thus: 'All invitations must proceed from heaven perhaps; perhaps it is futile for men to initiate their own unity, they do but widen the gulfs between them by the attempt. So at all events thought old Mr Graysford and young Mr Sorley.'[5]

In the profoundest sense, Forster's elusiveness is a quality of his mind – a mind at once humanistic and sceptical. 'I do not believe in belief,' he proclaims in his best-known essay, before proceeding to tell us what exactly he does believe in: tolerance, good temper, sympathy; personal relationships ('starting from them, I get a little order into the contemporary chaos'); an 'aristocracy of the sensitive, the considerate and the plucky'.[6] These are values, as Forster realizes, more applicable to private life than to public. But as a human being and a humanist, he is drawn both to private life and to public – to what Rickie Elliot, his young protagonist in *The Longest Journey*, calls 'the great world'. He recognizes the claims of friendship and institutions; he knows that we cannot escape, and should not seek to escape, the opportunities and responsibilities that the world affords.

Unlike nineteenth-century novelists, most of whom also recognized the claims of private and public life, Forster, in common with many twentieth-century writers, sees a fundamental division between the two realms. For most nineteenth-century novelists, there was no such necessary division. In the world of nineteenth-century fiction, a publicly acknowledged code of moral values is assumed by author and reader to be fixed and valid. Characters who are, or hope to be, happy observe the code. Those who violate it, do so at their peril.

---

[5] *A Passage to India*, chapter 4, p. 37. Harcourt, Brace, New York, 1952.
[6] 'What I Believe', in *Two Cheers for Democracy*, p. 73. Harcourt, Brace, New York, 1951.

So long as Jane Austen's *Emma* fails to accommodate her outlook and actions to this public sense of propriety, she is doomed to suffer a series of shocks and setbacks. But as soon as she is fully led to realize her errors and begins to align her values with the best ones of her society, she is rewarded with the proposal of Mr Knightley, the man who embodies in the highest degree the best elements of the moral order. For Jane Austen, as for Immanuel Kant, there is no necessary difference between the moral law within and that without. Her limited universe is all of a piece.

Forster's universe is divided. Living in a larger, less inte- *divided* grated world, he sees a fundamental dichotomy between *world* public life and private, between the aims and needs of society and those of the individual. Society needs government, an order, so to speak, imposed from without and, from Forster's point of view, largely inimical to the deeper needs of the individual. The individual, on the other hand, needs the satisfactions that can best be met through personal relationships and the claims of the inner life. The difference, in this respect, between Forster's vision and Jane Austen's can be illustrated by *A Room with a View*, Forster's most Jane-Austenlike novel. Whereas Emma is morally and psychologically ready to marry Mr Knightley only when she has reconciled her aims with her society's and accepted its implicit guiding code, Lucy can marry George only by turning her back on Summer Street and, in effect, rejecting its standards. For Lucy, as for her creator, the satisfactions of the inner life are incompatible with a completely integrated relationship with the outer.

Feeling himself to be in a world divided between the claims of the outer life and the inner, an individual might – especially if blest with a private income, as Forster was – choose to foster his inner life and avoid as far as possible the jarring claims of the outer. It is a tempting choice, and there is no question that Forster saw its attraction, for there is a strong escapist element in much of his fiction. In 'The Story of a Panic', the boy Eustace, under the sway of Pan, escapes the world of his elders. Rickie Elliot finds in the dell at Madingley a refuge from the uncomprehending world without. Maurice and Scudder flee to the greenwood. The elderly Mr Lucas tries to remain for the rest of his life at the Khan in Plataniste. Mrs Moore yearns to retire 'into a cave of my own'. Forster, however, was too curious about the world and saw too clearly the legitimacy of its claims to be satisfied with an escapist or epicurean fostering of the inner life. 'Will it really profit us so much,' he asks in *The Longest Journey*, 'if we save our souls and lose the whole world?' The question implies a correlative one, which haunts his fiction. To what extent can we save our souls and have the whole world? How far, in other words, are the claims of the inner life reconcilable with those of the outer?

If Forster is sometimes evasive, it is basically because he does not know how far such reconciliation is possible. Unlike the nineteenth-century novelist whose assured tone derives in great measure from his subscription to a publicly acknowledged code of values, Forster, without such a code, is tentative and exploratory. Will Dr Aziz and Cyril Fielding ever be able to reconcile the claims of their inner lives with those of the world? The last words of *A Passage to India* are Forster's only answer, and as well as any they convey that note of uncertainty that so often marks his voice: 'No, not yet...No, not there.'

II

The exploratory character of Forster's fiction is thematically suggested through its pervasive emphasis on travel. Most of the central characters travel, whether to a foreign country, a purely imaginary realm, or to various places within England itself. Philip Herriton and Lucy Honeychurch go to Italy; Rickie Elliot's very life, which is conceived as a 'longest journey', takes him from Sawston to public school and Cambridge, and to his aunt's estate in Wiltshire; Helen and Margaret Schlegel visit Germany, Hertfordshire and Wales; Maurice, like Rickie, goes from his suburban home to public school and Cambridge. Later, he visits his friend Clive

Durham's country estate, where, again like Rickie, he forms a crucial relationship with a young man. Mrs Moore and Adela Quested travel to India. The central characters in most of the short stories also travel. One thinks, for instance, of Miss Raby in Vorta, of Mr Lucas in Greece, of Lionel Marchbanks enroute to India, of the boy who boards the celestial omnibus, and of the pedestrian who, tired of walking, crawls through to the other side of the hedge.

All of these travellers visit places that yield them a new order of experience – an experience, that is to say, that lies beyond their normal range of activity and expectation. Their fundamental problem is to assimilate the new experience and accommodate it to their accustomed world.

Although varied in age and temperament, Forster's travellers are inwardly sensitive, and receptive to new places and people. Like Forster himself, they are generally products of a privileged middle-class upbringing, but being more endowed than the average man with imagination and sympathy, they are more likely to arrive at a fuller understanding of themselves and the world, and a fuller articulation of the life within them. Nevertheless, as is the case with most travellers, their receptiveness to the new is usually checked by the possession of certain values and attitudes derived from their class and culture. For all his love of Italy, Philip is a snob – a condition that prompts his objection to Lilia's marriage and inhibits his friendship with Gino. Maurice's love for Scudder, Rickie's for Stephen, and Lucy's for George, are also inhibited by their snobbery. Mrs Moore, of course, is no snob. Her problem with India stems partly from her age and ill-health, but more importantly from the fact that the country fails to conform to her English norms and her Christian-humanist sense of order. Whatever their outlook, all of Forster's travellers are to some extent pulled in contrary directions: toward the new experiences that travel brings and toward the world of familiar norms and values.

In their divided impulses, Forster's travellers resemble those in romantic allegory – Bunyan's Christian, for example, or

Spenser's Sir Guyon, who, venturing forth in search of spiritual fulfilment, are subject to forces that help or impede them in their quest, such forces (e.g. the Slough of Despond, the Bower of Bliss) being external counterparts of elements in the travellers' own natures. Forster's travellers differ from such figures in two respects: they are more highly individualized and they are not, at least in the conventional sense, heroic. The early protagonists – Philip, Rickie, and Lucy – are, in fact, unagressive, unsure of themselves, and consequently easily muddled by the play of stronger forces. But like the central figures in romantic allegory, Forster's travellers are in search of fulfilment and subjected in the course of their journeys to forces (characters, institutions, places) that help or impede them. Like traditional allegorists, moreover, Forster is inclined to conceive these forces in antithetical terms. On the one hand, Sawston, public schools, Herbert Pembroke and Mrs Herriton – the forces that check the traveller's receptiveness to what is new; on the other, Italy, Cambridge, Gino and Stephen Wonham – the forces that invite him to discover and fulfil what is new within himself, his life-enhancing instincts and feelings. *Howards End* and *A Passage to India* are more complex in structure and vision than the earlier novels, but their antithetical elements are still sharply drawn. In *Howards End*, the Schlegel sisters support the inner life; the Wilcoxes (with the notable exception of Ruth) the outer; both modes of life – as Margaret Schlegel comes to realize – being incomplete without the other. In Forster's last novel, the orderly, administrative minds of the English are opposed to the vital complexities of India; man's desire for ultimate meaning is opposed to a devastating spiritual nihilism. Throughout all six of the novels and in most of the short stories, the forces that would impose order from without are opposed to those that promote order within.

Between these antitheses the travellers move, trying to reconcile the forces' conflicting claims with their own psychological needs. Lucy would like both Summer Street and George. Margaret does not want to abandon her way of life, but to connect it to the world of business. Maurice does not really want to give up his career, and searches desperately for some way of reconciling its claims with those of his private life. And Mrs Moore would like to accommodate into a single vision her Christian universe and her experience of India.

Qualifying the allegorical aspect of Forster's fiction is its moral realism. Unlike such allegorists as Spenser and Bunyan for whom, in an age of more moral assurance than our own, good and evil were separate and distinct, Forster sees them as inextricably mixed. He is endowed, like Rickie Elliot, with the 'Primal Curse', which is not 'the knowledge of good and evil, but the knowledge of good-and-evil'. Even the antithetical forces affecting the travellers are seldom simply good or bad. Sawston may repress the free spirit, but, as Lilia Herriton realizes too late, it allows the majority of its inhabitants to lead pleasant, useful, well-ordered lives. It is the home not only of Philip's shrewish and calculating mother, but of Caroline Abbott, the well-intentioned young woman he grows to love. Italy may encourage the free spirit, but only for about half the human race: women, as Lilia again discovers, are far more repressed there than in Sawston. Gino, moreover, may be vital and charming; but he is also cunning, materialistic, and capable of cruelty. George Emerson has a morose and pessimistic streak that offsets his spontaneity and vitality. And Summer Street and Windy Corner, for all their limited view of life, have a warmth and beauty that Lucy leaves with regret.

Forster's moral realism is also displayed in the structure of his plots. The protagonists are involved in a network of good-and-evil. Helen Schlegel's attempt to help Leonard Bast leads by a chain of circumstances to Leonard's murder, which in turn contributes to Margaret's success in settling peacefully with her family at Howards End. As in life, failure or triumph in a Forster novel partly depends on circumstances beyond the individual's control.

In their drive toward self-fulfilment and their attempt to reconcile into a single vision the disparate elements of their experience, Forster's travellers are surrogates for Forster himself. As a man he would like to integrate his inner needs with outer facts. As an artist he would ideally like to weld into a unifying vision his experience of inner and outer life, art to Forster being chiefly valuable because it possesses 'internal harmony' and presents a vision of order to 'a permanently disarranged planet'.[7] The modern world, however, as Forster sees it, is recalcitrant to art, or at least to the art of the novelist who aspires to convey its richness and complexity. It is a multifarious and divided world – divided nationally, racially, ideologically; and, even more fundamentally, divided between private life and public, inner life and outer. 'How can the mind take hold of such a country?' he asks of India – a question that applies even more forcefully to the world as a whole.

Only in a limited and still integrated world could a novelist command the single vision – the world, for example, of rural England as Margaret saw it from Howards End. 'In these English farms, if anywhere,' she muses, looking out over the fields of Hertfordshire, 'one might see life steadily and see it whole'; see, that is, with the classical vision no longer applicable to the world at large. 'It is impossible,' declares Forster, 'to see modern life steadily and see it whole.'[8] Taken, then, as a group, Forster's travellers project his wish to explore the world and reflect it in fiction as deeply and comprehensively as his experience permits. At the same time they express his search as a man and artist for some way of harmonizing the values of public and private life.

III

Although Forster's acute sense of division between public and private life is probably shared by most of the major writers of the present century, it was almost certainly aggravated by his homosexuality. His early novels and stories appeared less than ten years after Wilde had been committed to prison for sodomy, and English attitudes toward the

[7] 'Art for Art's Sake', in *Two Cheers for Democracy*, p. 93. Harcourt, Brace, New York, 1951.
[8] *Howards End*, chapter 18, p. 158. Abinger Edition, 1973.

'unmentionable' practice had not perceptibly changed in the meantime. Throughout most of Forster's lifetime homosexuality, even among consenting adults, remained a crime. Not surprisingly, then, a homosexual was almost bound to feel cut off from the surrounding world of what passed for sexual normalcy. A basic and obsessional feature of his private life had to be guarded.

Forster's homosexuality almost certainly exercised a profound influence on his fiction. To begin with, there are, of course, one novel, *Maurice*, and eight short stories dealing directly with homosexuality. The first version of *Maurice* was written in 1913–14, between the publication of *Howards End* and *A Passage to India*; and the eight short stories between about 1922 and 1958;[9] most of them, that is, considerably after Forster was generally supposed to have given up the writing of fiction.

Taken as a whole, the novel and stories render in homosexual terms the major themes and concerns of the heterosexual fiction. Most of the protagonists go to places beyond their everyday sphere of activity where they are introduced to a new order of experience – to wit, homosexuality. Almost without exception,[10] Maurice and the principal characters in the stories are seduced, and in one instance actually raped, into active homosexuality. Their most important homosexual liaison, furthermore, is invariably with someone different in class and outlook: Maurice with Scudder, a gamekeeper; the Reverend Pinmay with an African tribal chief; Sir Richard Conway with a milkman; Lionel March with a half-caste native; Marcian, of a patrician Roman family, with a Goth. Whatever such relationships may suggest about Forster's own sexual preferences, they afford the main character an opportunity to transcend, if only temporarily, the restraints imposed by his class and upbringing; just as, in the heterosexual fiction, the same

---

[9] For dating evidence see Oliver Stallybrass's introductions to *Maurice* and *The Life to Come* in the Abinger Edition.

[10] The one exception is Sir Richard Conway in 'Arthur Snatchfold', who, though 'addicted to [the female sex]', permits himself 'an occasional deviation'.

9

opportunity is afforded Philip and Rickie through their relationship with Gino and Stephen respectively, or Fielding and Mrs Moore through their friendship with Dr Aziz. The consistency, in fact, with which Forster's principal homosexual characters find satisfaction outside their own class throws an interesting light on some of the key relationships in the rest of his fiction.

Forster's homosexuality may help to account for his generally unconvincing portrayal of heterosexual feeling. Despite her declaration that she loves Gino 'crudely', Caroline Abbott seems about as passionate as a plate of custard. Can one imagine Margaret and Henry Wilcox enjoying sex, or even indulging in it? As a lover, or even a human being, George Emerson is about as believable as a robot. Forster's handling of homosexual love, on the other hand, is more explicit and frequently more convincing. To be sure, Maurice's passion for Scudder rings as false as Lucy's for George, for neither Scudder nor George comes alive. But Maurice's love for Clive Durham rings true, and so does the complex blending of love, apprehension, and sadism that marks Lionel March's feeling for Cocoanut. The friendship between Aziz and Fielding may not be homosexual, but it is much more alive than the tepid attachment between Adela and Ronny.

Forster's probable apprehension of being publicly branded homosexual may underlie the fact that, at the heart of every one of the novels, there is some incident, generally sexual, whose exposure would, or does, give rise to scandal. Kidnapping, murder, and illicit love are among the activities in which his genteel men and women become involved. The very choice of a cave as the site for a sexual fantasy that overturns an entire civil administration gains significance in the light of Forster's probable apprehension.

Forster's homosexuality, then, almost certainly exercised a strong influence on his choice of themes and incidents. Nevertheless, one should beware of exaggerating that influence. If the fiction reflected only the interests and temperament of a talented homosexual, it would have a very

INTRODUCTION

limited audience indeed. Obviously it reflects a great deal
more.

Its vision of a divided world with individuals trying to
accommodate inner needs to an outer life often inimical to
those needs, and of becoming unwittingly enmeshed in a
network of good-and-evil, is profoundly true for our time. The
spectacle of men and women in public life becoming caught,
perhaps through misguided loyalty, in forces beyond their
control, and of trying to cover up a potential scandal, is all too
familiar. On a reduced scale, that is what Forster's novels are
largely about.

The novels qualify Forster's assertion that he belongs to 'the
fag-end of Victorian liberalism',[11] for they yield no straightforward affirmation of the value of tolerance, good temper
and sympathy, and of the superiority of the private life to the
public. Rather they test those values in a largely illiberal world,
Forster's key travellers being basically liberal-minded people
trying, in the main, to assert their better impulses in circumstances often designed to frustrate and pervert them.

How do the travellers fare? For the most part reasonably
well, even though three of them – Rickie Elliot, Mrs Moore,
and Lionel March – are destroyed by their experiences. None
of them, furthermore, completely succeeds in reconciling his
new experiences with his inherited values and the demands
of the everyday world. Wounded in mind and body, but wiser,
Philip abandons his family to live by himself in London. Rickie
is killed, still unable at the time of his death to accept Stephen
for what he is. Lucy gains George but loses her home and
family. Margaret marries Henry Wilcox and becomes mistress
of Howards End; but with Henry spiritually exhausted and
the Wilcox clan disunited, the connection lacks vitality. To live
with Scudder, Maurice abandons his family and his career.
Adela returns to England, ridden with guilt for her conduct
in India. Aziz and Fielding are finally separated by forces
beyond their control.

Are the novels, then, pessimistic? Are the travellers'

[11] 'The Challenge of our Time', in *Two Cheers for Democracy*.

11

journeys a failure? Certainly not. There are, after all, other things that matter besides aiming for an improbable harmony between the inner life and the outer. For one thing, there is romantic adventure – the exhilaration and apprehension aroused by new experience – and there is love and friendship. These things the travellers gain; and with them a richer sense of themselves and the world. And that, after all, is the beginning of wisdom.

1

Where Angels Fear to Tread

A socially preposterous marriage between a middle-class English widow and an Italian youth ten years her junior that culminates in kidnapping, homicide, and physical torture – this is the material out of which Forster weaves his first novel. The most patently melodramatic of the six, *Where Angels Fear to Tread* is as laced with implausibility as an Elizabethan tragedy and, like the latter, requires of the modern reader a generous suspension of disbelief. No modern family – and probably few Edwardian ones – would assume the proprietary interest in a widowed daughter-in-law and her child that the Herritons assume in Lilia and Irma. No modern daughter-in-law would for one minute tolerate such an interest. And if she chose to remarry, whether a foreigner or otherwise – the choice, she would firmly insist, would be her own business. That her former in-laws, moreover, would actually try, after her death in childbirth, to 'rescue' her baby from its foreign father, even to the point of kidnapping it, is hard enough to believe. But grant the kidnapping and the consequent accidental death of the infant, what are we to think when the child's grief-stricken father not only refuses to report the crime to the police but almost immediately forgives the kidnappers?

The novel's implausibilities, however, are not simply attributable to a cavalier disregard for realism. Rather they stem from Forster's instinct for allegory. In traditional allegory the clash of simplified characters embodying absolute moral values almost inevitably leads to far-fetched incidents. And so it is in *Where Angels Fear to Tread*, where the supporting characters and settings generally express clear-cut moral alternatives.

Mrs Herriton and her daughter Harriet embody respectability; the mother shrewd, cunning, and strong-willed – bent on preserving at any cost the family reputation; the daughter a Protestant prude, zealous on behalf of what she conceives to be her duty and that of others. They live, with Harriet's brother Philip, in Sawston, a repressively respectable London suburb.

Antithetically opposed to the two women is Gino Carella, the Italian youth whom Lilia Herriton marries. One of Forster's most carefully drawn and convincing characters, he is sensuous, hedonistic, shiftless and sociable; capable of tenderness and brutality; an embodiment of some of the vital contradictions that Forster discerned in the Italian spirit. Gino lives in Monteriano, an Italian hill-town that fosters a *douceur de la vie*.

Lilia's marriage to Gino sparks the main action – the two journeys that Philip Herriton makes to Italy, the first to try to prevent the marriage and the second, after Lilia's death, to bargain with Gino for custody of her baby. As a fun-loving widow Lilia had hoped to find in Italy and marriage a freedom that she had been denied in Sawston. But she is doomed to disappointment. Gino, who marries Lilia for her money, is too socially insecure to extend to his wife the freedom which, as a man, he takes for granted, with the result that Lilia perishes on the vine some months before she dies in childbirth. Forster's account of her married life is especially vivid.

When Philip goes to Italy he is confronted with compelling alternatives, either to succumb to his mother's repressive values and Sawston's, or to embrace Gino's vitality and Italy's and thereby be 'saved'. Philip's problem stems from his character. A cultivated and intelligent youth, he has already been to Italy before the novel opens and fallen in love with its beauty and history. Consequently, he falsely regards himself as superior to Sawston, at which, having failed to reform it, he directs his wit and humour. But for all his superior air, Philip is a snob, and just as bound as his mother and sister by notions of social caste. He is also unaggressive and indecisive; hence an easy tool for his mother's use. He sees the world as a show at which he is a spectator. Philip has much in common with his creator and with such sensitive Forsterian types as Rickie Elliot and Cecil Vyse; and in his self-conscious, slightly cynical sense of his own inadequacies, he anticipates Eliot's Prufrock.[1] His main handicap, at the start of the novel, is an undeveloped heart, which inhibits him from bridging barriers of class and culture to respond to purely human appeals. To develop his heart, he must be introduced to a new order of experience; and this means Italy, a country that, although he has been there once, he knows only as a romantic vista.

Philip's two journeys to Italy in the course of the action might be entitled, respectively, 'Disillusionment' and 'Salvation'. From Caroline Abbott, Lilia's young travelling companion, he learns on his first arrival in Monteriano the shocking truth that the man to whom Lilia is allegedly engaged is not even 'Italian nobility', as Caroline indicated by telegram, but the son of a dentist:

A dentist! A dentist at Monteriano. A dentist in fairyland! False teeth and laughing gas and the tilting chair at a place which knew the Etruscan League, and the Pax Romana, and Alaric himself, and the Countess Matilda, and the Middle Ages, all fighting and holiness, and the Renaissance, all fighting and beauty! He thought of Lilia no longer. He was anxious for himself: he feared that Romance might die. (32)[2]

Philip's meeting with Gino does nothing to relieve his distress. The Italian is familiar and vulgar, and accompanies his mirthful announcement that he and Lilia are already married by pushing Philip onto the bed.

Disillusioned with Italy but otherwise 'aesthetically intact', Philip returns to England to resume an existence whose calm is shattered only after Lilia's death when her nine-year-old daughter, Irma, begins to get postcards, fraught with potential

[1] In the MS of the novel in King's College Library, Cambridge, there is a long sentimental passage in which Forster reminisces about some of the friends he made in Italy. He then remarks, 'So it was with Philip, my true and tried acquaintance: who on this occasion, as on so many others, feels and behaves as I do.'

In his interview for the *Paris Review* (Spring 1953) Forster confesses to the resemblance between Philip, Rickie Elliot, Cecil Vyse, and himself.

[2] All page references in *Where Angels Fear to Tread* are from the Arnold, 1969 edition.

embarrassment to the Herritons, from her 'lital brother'. Irma lets the cat out of the bag by boasting at school about her newly discovered relation; and Caroline Abbott, feeling guilty for having encouraged Lilia to marry Gino and thereby prepared the way for her death, threatens to go, if necessary, to Italy to try to bring the child back to England. Not one to be exposed by Caroline if she can help it, Mrs Herriton sends a diplomatic letter to Gino offering to bring up his son in Sawston if he would only hand over Lilia's money and undertake never to see him again. His mother's object, as Philip sees, 'was to prevent Miss Abbott interfering with the child at all costs, and if possible to prevent her at a small cost. Pride was the only solid element in her disposition. She could not bear to seem less charitable than others.' (98–9) When Gino returns a flowery but nonetheless firm refusal to give up his son, Mrs Herriton decides to dispatch Philip and Harriet to Monteriano to see what personal diplomacy might accomplish.

When Philip and Harriet reach Monteriano, they find Caroline already there. She has come, she tells them, to spy on them, and to get the child if they should fail. Despite his role, Philip feels largely indifferent to the expedition's outcome. He is there, in effect, to enjoy the show: 'Harriet, worked by her mother; Mrs Herriton, worked by Miss Abbott; Gino, worked by a cheque – what better entertainment could he desire?' (106) His essentially frivolous outlook contrasts with Caroline's wish to salve her guilt and Harriet's fierce Protestant determination to rectify what she considers a moral outrage – that Lilia's baby should remain in Italy to be raised by a virtual infidel. Yet however different their motives, the three travellers are united in one attitude, their failure to consider the baby as a human being. To all three he is simply a thing, a cause, a means to an end.

To resolve his plot and save his protagonist, Forster contrives a series of incidents and encounters in which Caroline finally plays a crucial role, that of mediatress between Philip and Gino. A bland character with hidden potentialities (cf. Mr Beebe in *A Room with a View*), she had always impressed Philip

16

as amiable but dull – a girl who devoted her energy to her amiable but dull father and to nameless charities on behalf of the Sawston poor. Then, when she and Philip had ridden up to London together by train, she showed herself in a new light by confessing that she, too, hated Sawston, and that it was this that had impelled her to urge Lilia to marry Gino. 'Without being exactly original, she did show a commendable intelligence, and though at times she was gauche and even uncourtly, he felt that here was a person whom it might be well to cultivate.' (83–4) Now, in Italy, she must be brought round to Gino's side before she can mediate between the two men.

Forster prepares the ground for her conversion by having her run into Gino before Philip and Harriet arrive in Monteriano. Gino expresses regret to her for his earlier rudeness to Philip – an apology that pleases Philip when he learns about it from Caroline. 'For an apology, which would have been intolerable eighteen months ago, was gracious and agreeable now.' (124) The way is now open for Philip and Gino to meet on neutral ground, and this Forster arranges in one of the novel's most memorable scenes, a night at the opera.

Here in the opera house, Forster suggests, is the democratic vitality of Italy that Philip has so far missed. He, Harriet and Caroline go there together. Gino and a group of his friends are in a box; the crowds are milling and talking. The opera, as in *Madame Bovary*, is 'Lucia di Lammermoor'. That Philip, who has always regarded life as a show at which he is a privileged spectator, should while attending an opera be pushed and jostled into life is one of the novel's finer ironies. Hands reach down from Gino's box and pull Philip up into it. He and Gino warmly greet each other and Philip meets his friends. 'Tradesmen's sons perhaps they were, or medical students, or solicitor's clerks, or sons of other dentists. There is no knowing who is who in Italy.' (137) Though the business that brings the English to Italy is far from over, the barrier erected by Lilia's marriage and Philip's snobbery has been tentatively bridged.

17

For Caroline, too, the evening has been a romantic one. Like Philip she has obtained more than a tourist's view of Italy; she has been touched by its life – a life that, as we shall learn later, seems to her to be chiefly embodied in Gino. But suddenly she is pricked by conscience. Recalling that her only comparable moment of happiness was the night when Gino and Lilia told her of their love, she is overcome with shame.

> She was here to fight against this place, to rescue a little soul who was innocent yet. She was here to champion morality and purity, and the holy life of an English home. In the spring she had sinned through ignorance; she was not ignorant now. 'Help me!' she cried, and shut the window as if there was magic in the encircling air. But the tunes would not go out of her head, and all night long she was troubled by torrents of music, and by applause and laughter, and angry young men who shouted the distich out of Baedeker:
>
>> 'Poggibonizzi, fatti in là,
>> Che Monteriano si fa città!'
>
> Poggibonsi was revealed to her as they sang – a joyless, straggling place, full of people who pretended. When she woke up she knew that it had been Sawston. (139)

Fearful that her determination to do her duty may fail, Caroline goes the next morning to Gino's house to bargain with him for the baby. A somewhat sentimental scene follows, suggestive of Lawrence, in which Caroline, seeing the baby for the first time, feels the force of the bond between father and son. Never till now, she realizes, has she regarded the child as a human being. 'It did not stand for a principle any longer. It was so much flesh and blood, so many inches and ounces of life...' (145) Her heart moved, she helps Gino wash the child, an act charged with symbolic implication: Caroline is not merely drawing closer to Gino, she is cleansing her own soul of the moral bugbears and false guilt that have inhibited her acceptance of so much that is vital and vitalizing.

As Lawrence might have done, Forster tries to endow the homely episode with transcendent significance. One is reminded, for instance, of the scene in which Elizabeth Bates washes the body of her dead husband in 'The Odour of Chrysanthemums' and of that in which Jack Fergusson dries the nearly drowned Mabel Pervin in 'The Horse Dealer's Daughter'. Holding the baby, Gino is 'Majestic...a part of Nature; in no ordinary love scene could he ever be so great.' (155) The child's limbs are agitated by 'some overpowering joy' and Caroline feels 'strangely exalted by the service' (156). When she holds the baby on her knee, Gino kneels beside her, his 'hands clasped before him', in a grouping that reminds Philip, when he enters the room, of 'the Virgin and Child, with Donor' (157).

Lawrence at his best would have been less overtly pictorial and rendered more fully than Forster the impact of the scene on the subliminal lives of the two adults. Nor would he at his best have been sentimental as Forster is when he asserts Gino's greatness and majesty, and intrudes upon the portrait of father and son a generalization of doubtful validity:

> He stood with one foot resting on the little body, suddenly musing, filled with the desire that his son should be like him, and should have sons like him, to people the earth. It is the strongest desire that can come to a man – if it comes to him at all – stronger even than love or the desire for personal immortality. All men vaunt it, and declare that it is theirs; but the hearts of most are set elsewhere. It is the exception who comprehends that physical and spiritual life may stream out of him for ever. (153)

The scene is crucial. As a result of her visit, Caroline falls in love with Gino – a fact to which she confesses only at the end of the novel – and abandons her wish to get the baby. Philip and Harriet must now act alone. Philip, however, despite his newly-acquired fellow feeling for Gino, still feels indifferent to the expedition's outcome (162). Something is needed to shock his complacency, and this is amply provided.

Without his knowledge, Harriet kidnaps the baby; and when the carriage in which she, Philip and the infant are riding collides with Caroline's and overturns, killing the child, Philip, nursing a broken arm, takes it upon himself to go to Gino and confess the crime. The ensuing scene is unmatched in Forster's fiction for sheer violence. Gino grapples Philip to the floor and twists his broken arm. Philip faints from pain. Coming to, he finds Caroline there. In her new role as mediatress, she comforts Gino for his son's death and reconciles the two men – an event that all three ritualistically celebrate by drinking the milk the maid had brought for the baby.

Philip is now reborn. Inspired by Caroline's goodness and overwhelmed with a sense of the evil to which he has contributed, he determines to try to be good. 'Quietly, without hysterical prayers or banging of drums, he underwent conversion. He was saved.' (192)

The rest is epilogue. In the final scene, aboard the train that is taking the three travellers out of Italy, Philip and Caroline discuss the past and future. Still strained by recent events, Philip has formed what promises to be an enduring friendship with Gino and fallen in love with Caroline. Like Forster's other early hero Rickie Elliot, he needs to love some embodiment of truth, beauty, and goodness; and such he has found, he feels, in the young woman beside him in the train's corridor. 'He had reached love by the spiritual path: her thoughts and her goodness and her nobility had moved him first, and now her whole body and all its gestures had become transfigured by them.' (196) He will reject Sawston, he tells Caroline, for 'London and work'. She will return to Sawston, she replies, and resume her old life, for 'all the wonderful things are over' (199). On the verge of proposing marriage, Philip must now learn the final truth in the complicated chain of events in which they have been involved – that she is physically and passionately in love with Gino, and that it was only the latter's failure to respond in kind ('he took me for a superior being – a goddess') that gave her the strength to play her mediating role. This shattering confession not only extends Philip's understanding; it heightens his veneration of the woman who has triumphed over her passions to reconcile the opposing parties. As the train nears the St Gothard tunnel, he and Caroline hurry back to close the windows of their compartment 'lest the smuts should get into Harriet's eyes'.

Like most of Forster's novels, *Where Angels Fear to Tread* poses the question of who, or what, is responsible for the events – Philip, who encouraged Lilia to visit Italy; Caroline, who urged her to marry Gino; Lilia and Gino for marrying; Mrs Herriton, who, prompted by pride and vanity, instigated the expedition to bring back the baby; Harriet, who kidnapped it; or Sawston or Italy, which embody subtle forces beyond anyone's control? Everyone of these elements contributes to the catastrophe and its aftermath; and it is Philip's realization of this that prompts his reflection, 'Life was greater than he had supposed, but it was even less complete. He had seen the need for strenuous work and for righteousness. And now he saw what a very little way those things would go.' (197) As Professor Godbole will later declare, 'When evil occurs, it expresses the whole of the universe';[3] an observation which, however applicable to the real world, is true in Forster's fictive one. We are caught in a web of moral forces, Forster suggests, whose end nobody can predict.

Forster heightens the novel's allegorical dimension by means of several symbolically suggestive features. The smuts that afflict Harriet's eyes are an obvious symbol. The St Gothard tunnel recalls innumerable romantic passageways between two worlds, one generally more desirable than the other. On the Italian side of the tunnel stands the Campanile of Airolo, an ironic emblem of aspiration that seems to Lilia, when she first sees it, to presage the future.

Forster's choice of a hilltown for the novel's principal setting may have been partly determined by its potentially purgatorial character. For it is Philip's purgatory, the place where he suffers the consequences of his moral indifference and attains to a higher vision. Looking with Caroline at one of the town's seventeen towers, he remarks, 'It reaches up to heaven and down to the other place...Is it to be a symbol of the town?' (126–7) Symbolically viewed Monteriano is a halfway house between hell and heaven. Its towers, its church, its patron saint combine to suggest its celestial aspirations; yet its life, as the novel so clearly shows, is capable of tapping demonic springs.

[3] *A Passage to India*, 178. Harcourt, Brace, New York, 1952.

If Monteriano is a purgatory, the little wood at the base of the hill on which the town is set recalls Dante's 'selva oscura', the dark forest in which the poet is lost at the beginning of the *Divine Comedy*. When Philip passes through the wood on his way to dissuade Lilia from marrying, he is, like Dante at the start of his pilgrimage, lost in error. He is morally muddled and misconceives both the nature of Italy and the circumstances that have directed him there. When Gino at lunch, eager to display his learning, recites the opening lines of the *Divine Comedy*, he unconsciously stresses the analogy between Dante's experience and Philip's; for the quotation, as Forster remarks, was 'more apt than he [Gino] supposed' (38). Cold and damp in the autumn of the following year, the little wood is the setting for the fatal climax of Philip's mistake, the place where the carriage overturns in the mud and the baby is killed. But when Philip first passes through it in spring, it is carpeted with violets. Preoccupied with the question of Lilia, Philip pays no attention to the flowers, which symbolically foreshadow his own regeneration.

Philip, of course, is no Dante. Idle and callow as he is at the beginning of the novel, he has none of the latter's moral passion or creative genuis; and where Dante was driven by a consuming love for Beatrice, Philip seems little more than a conscious reflex of his mother's will. Considering the gulf between the two men, it is ironic, then, that Philip himself appears to discern a Dantesque element in the novel's opening situation. 'Here beginneth the new life,' he remarks to his mother after Lilia's departure for Italy. The words translate Dante's 'Incipit Vita Nova', the statement that signals the sense of rebirth that his love for Beatrice had given to him. Though Philip does not apply the words to himself but to Lilia and Irma, they ironically apply to him too. Like Dante he will embark on a journey that leads, if not to the gates of heaven, at least to a higher plane of perception.

As different as Philip is from Dante, he does have two qualities that Forster attributes to Dante in his early essay on the Italian poet.[4] One is idealism, and the other a detachment from individuals. Forster remarks that Dante tended to look through people rather than at them, 'and through most of them he saw nothing, and through one of them he saw God'.[5] Philip is also detached from people. 'I seem fated to pass through the world without colliding with it or moving it,' he tells Caroline, 'and I'm sure I can't tell you whether the fate's good or evil. I don't die – I don't fall in love. And if other people die or fall in love they always do it when I'm just not there. You are quite right; life to me is just a spectacle...' (168) Dante's detachment from individuals was one source of his power. 'His standpoint is not in this world. He views us from an immense height, as a man views a plain from a mountain.'[6] By the end of the novel, Philip, too, is able to assume something of a cosmic perspective. 'You are the only one of us,' says Caroline, 'who has a general view of the muddle.' (165) Philip himself comes to feel – in words that anticipate those of the 'Dante' essay – that 'nobody but himself would ever see round it now. And to see round it he was standing at an immense distance.' (204)

In his capability of seeing round the experience Philip has acquired something of the power attributed to the classic artist of seeing life steadily and seeing it whole. It was a power to which Forster was obviously attracted, for many of his key characters – Rickie Elliot, Margaret Schlegel, Mrs Moore, and Professor Godbole, for example – try to achieve it. But it is a difficult power to reconcile with Forster's humanism, with his commitment to individuals and personal relationships; and none of his characters convincingly reconciles the two contraries.

Philip's difficulty in responding to the human as human emerges in his growing veneration for Caroline – a veneration suggestive of Dante's for Beatrice. Caroline achieves her apo-

[4] First published in *The Working Men's College Journal*, vol. 10 (February–April 1908), 261–4, 281–6, 301–6. Reprinted in *Albergo Empedocle and Other Writings*, ed. George H. Thomson (New York, 1971). Hereafter cited as Thomson.
[5] Thomson, p. 153.   [6] Thomson, p. 167.

theosis in the torture scene when Philip, recovering consciousness, finds the room 'full of light' and Caroline restoring
harmony.

All through the day Miss Abbott had seemed to Philip like a goddess, and
more than ever did she seem so now...Her eyes were open, full of infinite
pity and full of majesty, as if they discerned the boundaries of sorrow, and
saw unimaginable tracts beyond. Such eyes he had seen in great pictures but
never in a mortal. (192)

Caroline's effect on Philip's character is, on a lower level, as
salutary as Beatrice's on Dante's. Just as Beatrice felt moved
to recall Dante from a form of spiritual death, so Caroline
rebukes Philip for a passivity and moral indifference tanta-
mount to death. 'Oh, you appreciate me,' he burst out again.
'I wish you didn't. You appreciate us all – see good in all of
us. And all the time you are dead-dead-dead.' (168) Dante's
love for Beatrice, writes Forster, made him discipline his body
and soul that he might be worthy of the high thoughts to which
she led him.[7] Philip acquires 'an earnest desire to be good
through the example of this good woman' (192).

Yet surely Philip's worship of Caroline is no more flattering
to her womanhood than was Dante's, according to Forster, to
Beatrice's. 'Which seems to pay the truer homage – Dante
looking through Beatrice, or Othello looking at Desdemona;
Dante narrating the return of his lady to the angels, or King
Lear with Cordelia dead in his arms?'[8] The same sort of
question might be asked of Philip. Unable, finally, to distinguish the ideal from the real, he refuses to degrade Caroline
to the level of mere humanity. His eyes fixed on the Campanile
of Airolo as the train approaches the tunnel, he sees instead
'the fair myth of Endymion. This woman was a goddess to the
end.' (204)

Compared, of course, to Dante's austerely poetic vision,
Philip's deification of Caroline is a piece of sentimental extra-
vagance. We cannot take it as seriously as Philip himself takes
it or – the evidence suggests – as Forster means us to take it.
Although he sometimes regards him ironically, he also pro-

<hr />

[7] Thomson, p. 151.   [8] Thomson, p. 151.

jects much of himself into Philip. Forster shares Philip's feeling for art and beauty, his disposition to laugh at Sawston's pretensions, his need to detach himself from the world around him in order to understand it and, at the same time, to involve himself with others. He sympathizes with Philip's ethical and aesthetic idealism. Hence Philip's veneration of Caroline, extravagant though it may be, reflects Forster's own desire for some transcendant expression of truth and beauty.

The strain of romantic idealism that Forster, when he wrote his first novel, shared with Philip sometimes betrays him into sentimentality – into a tendency to inflate a subject beyond the limits of its nature. Of Gino he asserts that 'he was that glorious invariable creature, a man' (69) and of Lilia, unhappy in her marriage, he declares – perhaps half facetiously, but only half – that 'not Cordelia nor Imogen more deserves our tears' (70). Gino with his son is, as we have seen, 'majestic... a part of Nature; in no ordinary love scene could he ever be so great' (155). And Philip's final assessment of Caroline is one that Forster seems to want us to take seriously. Such passages as these, which reflect Forster's occasional inability to look objectively at his subject, are blemishes in a generally well-controlled and penetrating book.

Despite the seriousness of its theme and the violence and suffering with which it deals, *Where Angels Fear to Tread* is a comic novel, infused with wit and gaiety. Forster's next novel, *The Longest Journey*, is more personal and more tragic.

What!
AW say
not

2

The Longest Journey

Forster's second novel, *The Longest Journey*, is the most personal of the five and the least popular. Yet, although it has faults that partly explain its comparative unpopularity, it is a subtle and searching examination into a problem that has always engaged Forster, both as a humanist and novelist, the relationship between vision and truth and between symbol and reality. 'No one,' as K. W. Gransden has said, 'can simultaneously dislike it and care for Forster as a writer.'[1]

Rickie Elliot's longest journey is the journey of his life, taking him from the suburb in which he was born and where, during his childhood, his parents die to public school and on to Cambridge University; from there to a public school in Sawston (Forster's recurrent and repressive suburb), where he serves as an assistant master; and finally to Cadover, his Aunt Emily Failing's estate in Wiltshire, not far from which he falls victim to sudden and accidental death. His largely unhappy life is marked by his marriage to an unsympathetic woman, Agnes Pembroke; by the death of their one child, a daughter, in infancy; and, most significantly, by the revelation that his aunt's ward Stephen Wonham, a youth whom he dislikes, is his illegitimate half-brother. Assuming Stephen to be the son of his father, whom he hated, Rickie tries to ignore the young man and his relationship to him. His action, as is almost inevitable in Forster's novels, provokes a muddle from which Rickie is rescued only when, learning that Stephen is not his father's son at all but his beloved mother's, he tries to accept him. But the attempt leads to disaster, for Rickie persists in regarding Stephen not as a fellow man with a life of his own but as a living symbol of his dead mother. But Stephen refuses

[1] K. W. Gransden, *E. M. Forster* (Writers and Critics series), p. 38. Edinburgh and London, 1962.

to act like a symbol. One evening, breaking his word to Rickie that he would not drink, he gets drunk and falls across the railway tracks in the path of an oncoming train. Shattered by Stephen's conduct, Rickie wearily does 'a man's duty' and drags him from the tracks. The train runs over Rickie's knees and he dies shortly afterwards, broken in body and spirit. Stephen, on the other hand, the natural child and a child of nature, survives to marry, beget a daughter, and perhaps to guide the future of England.

The Longest Journey is thus a dark novel – all the darker, in fact, for the number of sudden deaths that occur in it and the air of fatality that surrounds the hero. Born with a lameness derived from his father's side of the family, physically weak besides, and raised by his mother in solitude and loneliness, Rickie seems predestined to failure. His unhappy marriage echoes the unhappiness that subsisted between his mother and father. His daughter's lameness echoes his own. Like Ibsen's Oswald Alving, he becomes haunted by the 'ghosts' of his own prehistory. No other of Forster's novels is so fatalistic; in no other does the hero's unhappiness seem so hopeless.

Yet despite the fact that he is largely a victim of circumstances, his longest journey expresses his search for what in the novel is called reality – for some mode of existence that fulfils his imaginative and emotional needs and reflects the concerns of what Rickie vaguely refers to as 'the great world' (76).[2] Rickie's search is also Forster's. Rickie too wants to write, and as a Cambridge undergraduate has in fact written some mythological tales like some of Forster's. But these stories, as he comes to realize after he falls in love with Agnes, fail to accord with his growing experience. 'You see, a year or two ago,' he tells Agnes, 'I had a great idea of getting into touch with nature...It's funny enough now, but it wasn't funny then, for I got in such a state that I believed, actually believed, that Fauns lived in a certain double hedgerow near the Gog Magogs, and one evening I walked a mile sooner than go through it alone.'

[2] All page references in *The Longest Journey* are from the New Directions, Norfolk, Conn., edition.

(86) But the fact that Rickie's fantasies no longer reflect his experience confronts him with a problem: how can he relate his growing experience to his sense of values? how can he assimilate his experience to his imagination? how much experience does one need before one begins to write? We must drink the cup of experience, Forster warns,

> or we shall die. But we need not drink it always. Here is our problem and our salvation. There comes a moment – God knows when – at which we can say, 'I will experience no longer. I will create. I will be an experience.' But to do this we must be both acute and heroic. For it is not easy, after accepting six cups of tea, to throw the seventh in the face of the hostess. (75)

Rickie's journey, then, is a search for some way of harmonizing his imaginative and emotional life with the facts of experience. But before the novel has developed beyond the first chapter, it is clear that he will have more difficulty than most people.

With a group of fellow undergraduates, he is engrossed, at the beginning of chapter 1, in a conversation about a cow. They are in Rickie's college rooms, the time is dusk, and they are discussing the old philosophical chestnut as to whether something exists if there is no one to perceive it. 'The cow,' declares Stewart Ansell, 'is there.' The cow, he means, exists, even though no one in the room can see her. Some of the undergraduates disagree with Ansell. The cow, they argue, only exists as she is perceived. As for Rickie, he cannot make up his mind, and characteristically begins to daydream.

> Either way it was attractive. If she was there, other cows were there too. The darkness of Europe was dotted with them, and in the far East their flanks were shining in the rising sun. Great herds of them stood browsing in pastures where no man came nor need ever come, or plashed knee-deep by the brink of impassable rivers. And this, moreover, was the view of Ansell. Yet Tilliard's view had a good deal in it. One might do worse than follow Tilliard, and suppose the cow not to be there unless oneself was there to see her. A cowless world, then, stretched round him on every side. Yet he had only to peep into a field, and, click! it would at once become radiant with bovine life. (13)

The cow question suddenly becomes less academic with the entrance of Agnes Pembroke. Rickie has invited her and her

brother Herbert up for the weekend, and, again quite characteristically, has forgotten to meet them at the station. Agnes
is annoyed. 'Wicked, intolerable boy!' she exclaims, 'wicked,
abominable, intolerable boy! I'll have you horsewhipped'
(14–15), and more words to the same effect. Curiously, Ansell
refuses to shake hands with her or even acknowledge her
presence when Rickie introduces him; and later, when Rickie
asks him to explain his rudeness, he replies, 'I saw no one
. . .She was not really there.' (26–7) He then proceeds,

Did it never strike you that phenomena may be of two kinds: *one*, those which
have a real existence, such as the cow; *two*, those which are the subjective
product of a diseased imagination, and which, to our destruction, we invest
with the semblance of reality? If this never struck you, let it strike you now.
(27)

But his warning – and prophecy – go unheeded. To Rickie,
she was more than there. Overwhelmed by her manner and
appearance, he had seen not simply a handsome girl but a girl
'like an empress' (27), an illusion no doubt enhanced by the
strains of 'Das Rheingold' which one of the undergraduates
had been banging out on the piano when she came in.

Rickie, then, as the opening chapter makes clear, is more
at home in the world of fantasy than fact. A flashback to his
childhood in chapter 2 gives an indication why. Lame and
solitary, with only his mother to care for him, he had naturally
turned in upon himself and developed his imagination.

He would conduct solitary conversations, in which one part of him asked and
another part answered. It was an exciting game, and concluded with the
formula: 'Good-bye. Thank you. I am glad to have met you. I hope before
long we shall enjoy another chat.' And then perhaps he would sob for
loneliness, for he would see real people – real brothers, real friends – doing
in warm life the things he had pretended. 'Shall I ever have a friend?' he
demanded at the age of twelve. 'I don't see how. They walk too fast. And
a brother I shall never have.' (35)

Reality, then, for Rickie, consists of two aspects, inner and
outer, which ideally should be integrated.

In chapter 1, the point is illuminated by the diagram that
Ansell is drawing when Rickie asks him to explain his rudeness
to Agnes. Consisting of a square within which is a circle, within

which is a square, and so on in ever diminishing size, it is a mandala, an age-old symbol of unity and harmony in the material and phenomenal worlds. The circles symbolizing – as in Christian iconography – the celestial and the visionary, and the squares the mundane and the practical, the total configuation points to Rickie's desire for a total, integrated reality. 'Are they real?' asks Rickie, looking at the configuration of squares and circles. 'The inside one is,' replies Ansell, 'the one in the middle of everything, that there's never room enough to draw.' (27) He means that reality, both spiritual and material, derives from one ultimate source or centre; but whether that source or centre is spiritual, material, or both, no one can say. That Ansell should draw the diagram is as appropriate as his support of the cow's objective existence and of Agnes's subjective one; for he is Rickie's chief guide on his longest journey, recalling him to the path of objective fact when he becomes mired in fantasy.

The diagram also points to Rickie's search for a single embodiment of the good and the beautiful, some peg, as Ansell puts it, on which he can hang 'all the world's beauty' (96). A visionary idealist, he readily endows certain places and people with absolute beauty and goodness. The dell at Madingley, for instance, where he spends many happy hours alone or with his friends, seems to him 'a kind of church...his holy place', to which a sign might appropriately point 'This way to Heaven' (28–9). Later, the Wiltshire Downs exercise a similar spell on him. His idealization of Agnes, already apparent in chapter 1, achieves an apotheoisis when he comes upon her and her fiance, Gerald Dawes, locked in a passionate embrace. The moment is for him 'symbolic': a moment imaginatively transfigured, when essential reality seems to stand revealed and time itself to be transcended. Watching the lovers embrace, Rickie feels himself to be 'looking down coloured valleys', at 'pinnacles of virgin snow', and then to be standing at the very 'springs of creation' hearing the 'primeval monotony' (52). Agnes, accordingly, becomes one of the pegs on which he hangs all the world's beauty.

Another peg, before Agnes, was 'humanity'. A starry-eyed
undergraduate, he had aspired to love mankind; for like
Shelley, his favourite poet, he did not want to travel 'the
longest journey' with 'one sad friend, perhaps a jealous foe',
and commend the rest of humanity to 'cold oblivion'; although
that, of course, was to be his fate. Falling in love with Agnes,
however, he comes to care less about others. Shelley's lines
from 'Epipsychidion', of whose sentiment he had once ap-
proved, now strike him as 'a little inhuman' (147). 'I'm beginning to see,' he tells Agnes, 'that the world has many people
in it who don't matter. I had time for them once. Not now'
– to which Forster adds the laconic comment, 'There was only
one gate to the kingdom of heaven now.' (142) Later, with the
deterioration of his marriage, his mother becomes the peg on
which he hangs the world's beauty. She is his 'mater dolorosa',
to whom, after his daughter's death, he prays in his misery,
begging to be freed of the 'ghosts' that haunt him, 'the faces
that frothed in the gloom – his aunt's, his father's, and, worst
of all, the triumphant face of his brother' (222).

But just as Rickie transfigures his mother and earlier Agnes
into embodiments of the good, so as easily he degrades
Stephen into a symbol of sin. He was 'the fruit of sin', the
son, as Rickie supposes, of his father; 'therefore he was sinful'
(161).

Rickie's revulsion at Stephen's bastardy reveals of course a
puritan element in his character – a puritanism evident in his
initial dislike of Stephen when he and Agnes visit Cadover.
Stephen, it is at once apparent, is the antithesis of Rickie. A
free spirit, he takes the world for granted and enjoys himself
in it as best he can. Earthy, good-natured, ill-educated, and
coarse, he is happiest out of doors, farming or riding over the
Wiltshire fields. Rickie is put off by his coarseness from the
start, and when they go riding together and stop at a public
house and Stephen drinks beer with a soldier and tells raucous
stories, Rickie sinks his head lower and lower as each wave of
vulgarity bursts over him. One of these stories, 'a sordid
village scandal – such as Stephen described as a huge joke –

sprang from certain defects in human nature, with which he was theoretically acquainted. But the example! He blushed at it like a maiden lady, in spite of its having a parallel in a beautiful idyll of Theocritus.' (131) Stephen's Hellenism is genuine. Rickie's is bookish and theoretical. More deeply ingrained is his puritanism, which makes it hard for him to drink the 'cup of experience', to assimilate those facts of life without which human beings, and novelists, must be narrow and precious.

The three sections into which *The Longest Journey* is divided – Cambridge, Sawston, and Wiltshire – mark the three major kinds of experience to which Rickie is exposed in the course of his adult life. Cambridge, as Forster presents it, is humanistic. Its atmosphere encourages learning and friendship. Rickie makes friends here, reads classics, talks philosophy, and is happy for the first and only time in his life. His familiar rooms are his home, a shelter – like the dell at Madingley – from the outer world which, both of his parents being dead, affords him no place to settle. To be sure, there are 'sets' at Cambridge – the athletes or 'beefy set', and Rickie and his non-athletic, cultivated friends who generally consider themselves 'saved'. Rickie would like to break down the barriers dividing the sets; but for that ambition his friends tease him.

Yet with the advent of Agnes, Rickie comes to feel that Cambridge, for all its warmth and intellectual vitality, is narrow. Agnes and her brother Herbert represent Sawston, and a way of life that has nothing to do with Cambridge. When Rickie visits Sawston during the holiday, he has two 'symbolic moments' that seem to him more 'real' than anything he has known at Cambridge. The first is his vision of Agnes and Gerald making love. The second is provoked by Gerald's sudden death ('he was broken up in a football match') and the sight of Agnes holding the dying youth in her arms. Moved by the spectacle, Rickie tells Agnes that she has got to 'mind' Gerald's death. 'It's the worst thing that can ever happen to you in all your life, and you've got to mind it – you've got to mind it. They'll come saying, "Bear up – trust to time." No,

no; they're wrong. Mind it.' (66) Rickie means that such privileged moments, whether of joy or anguish, are the essence of
life, the centre, so to speak, of Ansell's mandala; and only by
seizing and treasuring them can the spirit grow. Rickie himself
seizes and treasures the event. Hitherto his enthusiasms 'had
played on gods and heroes, on the infinite and the impossible,
on virtue and beauty and strength. Now, with a steadier
radiance, they transfigured a man who was dead and a woman
who was still alive.' (74)

His two 'symbolic moments', however, breed a dissatisfac-
tion with Cambridge. Returning after the holiday, he does not
discuss Gerald's death with his friend Ansell. 'Ansell could
discuss love and death admirably, but somehow he would not
understand lovers or a dying man.' And as for the dons, 'they
dealt with so much and they had experienced so little. Was
it possible he would ever come to think Cambridge narrow?'
(70) The subject of Cambridge's 'narrowness' recurs two years
later during Rickie's last summer term. 'Cambridge,' says
Rickie, 'is wonderful, but – it's so tiny. You have no idea – at
least, I think you have no idea – how the great world looks
down on it.' Rebuking his friend's English, Ansell replies:

There is no great world at all, only a little earth, for ever isolated from the
rest of the solar system. The earth is full of tiny societies, and Cambridge is
one of them. All the societies are narrow, but some are good and some are
bad – just as one house is beautiful inside and another ugly. Observe the
metaphor of the houses: I am coming back to it. The good societies say, 'I
tell you to do this because I am Cambridge.' The bad ones say, 'I tell you
to do that because I am the great world' – not because I am 'Peckham,' or
'Billingsgate,' or 'Park Lane,' but 'because I am the great world.' They lie.
And fools like you listen to them, and believe that they are a thing which does
not exist and never has existed, and confuse 'great,' which has no meaning
whatever, with 'good', which means salvation. Look at this great wreath: it'll
be dead to-morrow. Look at that good flower: it'll come up again next year.
Now for the other metaphor. To compare the world to Cambridge is like
comparing the outsides of houses with the inside of a house. No intellectual
effort is needed, no moral result is attained. You only have to say, 'Oh, what
a difference!' and then come indoors again and exhibit your broadened mind.
(77)

Ansell's reply, of course, accords both with Rickie's future
experience and with Forster's vision of a divided, multifarious

world. In his Introduction to the World's Classics edition of *The Longest Journey* published in 1960, Forster writes, 'I still endorse Ansell's denunciation of the Great World.' (xi)

Before going to Sawston, Rickie has two experiences that forever shatter the calm and security he has known at Cambridge, his engagement to Agnes and the revelation of his brotherhood with Stephen. Each event is connected with a symbolic moment and with one of those epiphanous spots so prominent in Forster's fiction; and the two events, seemingly separate, are ironically linked.

The engagement, which stems from the fact that Rickie impressed Agnes with his imaginative sympathy at the time of Gerald's death, is precipitated by their visit to the dell at Madingley during May Week of Rickie's last term. Forster's choice of setting is significant, for the dell is for Rickie a retreat from the uncertainties of life, a natural womb that partly compensates him for the loss of his mother. And in Agnes he finds a mother-substitute, as the ensuing scene suggests. Within the dell, he lays his head on her lap and succumbs to the symbolic moment.

it was neither June nor January. The chalk walls barred out the seasons, and the fir-trees did not seem to feel their passage. Only from time to time the odours of summer slipped in from the wood above, to comment on the waxing year. She bent down to touch him with her lips. (89)

But the kiss is too much for Rickie. He starts, a victim of conscience and sexual inhibition, and tries to recall Agnes to the memory of her symbolic moment with Gerald. 'What I said to you then is greater than what I say to you now. What he gave you then is greater than anything you will get from me.' (89) Within the dell, his head on Agnes's lap, Rickie is like an infant who wants protection from the world; and, as if he were an infant, Agnes tries to comfort him. 'She was frightened. Again she had the sense of something abnormal. Then she said, 'What is all this nonsense?' and folded him in her arms.' (89) The scene prefigures her dominant role in their marriage.

Rickie's second epiphany also takes place in a particular spot, the Cadbury Rings, a prehistoric tumulus not far from Cad-over, his aunt's estate in Wiltshire. Having quarrelled with Aunt Emily about the church service they had attended, he walks up to the Rings to enjoy the view and regain his temper; but presently he sees his aunt, with Agnes in tow, coming toward him in the pony carriage. Irritated with Rickie, she has decided to shock him. A detached, worldly, and rather mali-cious old lady, she likes to shock conventional people provided the chill is 'not infectious'. Thus she had shocked Agnes whom, acutely, she perceived to be a conventional girl, by introducing Stephen to her as one of her shepherds. ('Agnes smiled rather wildly...A shepherd in the drawing-room!') Now she will shock her puritan nephew and so revenge herself for his 'rudeness'.

As with the earlier epiphany, the setting is important. Re-calling both Ansell's mandala and the dell, the Rings consist of a bank of grass enclsoing a ring of turnips, enclosing a second bank of grass, enclosing a second ring of turnips, and in the middle a small tree. The spot reminds Rickie of the dell, for not only is the view of the outside world from it 'greatly diminished', but the arrival of Agnes at the Rings recalls her presence in the dell. This time, however, she stands on the outer barrier waiting for Rickie and his aunt to traverse the Rings alone; for in the morality drama now being staged, she represents illusion, 'the subjective product of a diseased imagination', and hence cannot cross to the tree in the centre, the tree of knowledge.

The ensuing scene is stagy but forceful. A church bell peals as Aunt Emily, relishing an Ibsenian desire to let in fresh air, leads Rickie toward the centre of the Rings, remarking as she does so that the place is 'full of ghosties', the spirits, that is, of the pagan soldiers who are buried there. Proceeding to exhume another sort of ghost, she drops a few seemingly casual references to 'your brother', which Rickie, seeing that Stephen is meant, at first attributes to a slip of the tongue. As they move toward the centre, the church bell stops pealing. (Being cracked, it had reminded Aunt Emily of Rickie.) Aunt

35

Emily's references to 'your brother' become more persistent; and suddenly, at the centre, the horror leaps at Rickie. Only a few minutes before, stirred by the thought of the dead soldiers and their modern descendants, he had romanticized the past and the notion of continuity. Now 'he was gazing at the past,... which gaped ever wider, like an unhallowed grave. Turn where he would, it encircled him. It took visible form: it was this double entrenchment of the Rings.' (151) Like Adela Quested and Mrs Moore in the Marabar Caves, he is overwhelmed with a claustrophobia and runs fainting for the exit. Before he can find it, he does faint. And the next thing he hears is his brother's voice, the voice of truth, summoning him to wake. Instinctively, but for only an instant, Rickie accepts the reality revealed by the symbolic moment and cries out to his brother. Then Agnes, the product of his imagination, moves in from the periphery of the Rings and clasps her lover to her breast. Saving him from the truth, she can now proceed, with Herbert's help, to manoeuvre him into a modern house of falsehood, Sawston School.

Sawston School, which marks the second stage of Rickie's journey, is false both because it espouses values of which Forster disapproves – such as *esprit de corps* and nationalism – and because, unlike Cambridge, a 'good society', it purports to be 'the world in miniature' (182). The key to its method is organization; and its chief organizer is Herbert Pembroke, Master of Dunwood House, and one of the prime goats in Forster's fiction.

If no organization existed, he would create one. If one did exist, he would modify it...The school caps, with their elaborate symbolism, were his; his the many-tinted bathing-drawers, that showed how far a boy could swim; his the hierarchy of jerseys and blazers. It was he who instituted Bounds, and call, and the two sorts of exercise-paper, and the three sorts of caning, and 'The Sawstonian', a bi-terminal magazine. His plump finger was in every pie. The dome of his skull, mild but impressive, shone at every master's meeting. He was generally acknowledged to be the coming man. (55)

Forster's account of the school in action contains some of his best satire. Here, for example, is the first-day's assembly,

rendered with a mock-heroic vigour and an eye for ironic
detail that recalls the art of Dickens and Fielding:

The room was almost full. The prefects, instead of lolling disdainfully in the
back row were ranged like councillors beneath the central throne. This was
an innovation of Mr Pembroke's. Carruthers, the head boy, sat in the middle,
with his arm round Lloyd. It was Lloyd who had made the matron too bright:
he nearly lost his colours in consequence. These two were grown up. Beside
them sat Tewson, a saintly child in spectacles, who had risen to this height
by reason of his immense learning. He, like the others, was a school prefect.
The house prefects, an inferior brand, were beyond, and behind came the
indistinguishable many. The faces all looked alike as yet – except the face of
one boy, who was inclined to cry. 'School,' said Mr Pembroke, slowly closing
the lid of the desk, – 'school is the world in miniature.' Then he paused, as
a man well may who has made such a remark. It is not, however, the intention
of this work to quote an opening address. Rickie, at all events, refused to be
critical: Herbert's experience was far greater than his, and he must take his
tone from him. Nor could any one criticize the exhortations to be patriotic,
athletic, learned, and religious, that flowed like a four-part fugue from Mr
Pembroke's mouth. He was a practised speaker – that is to say, he held his
audience's attention. He told them that this term, the second of his reign, was
the term for Dunwood House; that it behoved every boy to labour during it
for his house's honour, and, through the house, for the honour of the school.
Taking a wider range, he spoke of England, or rather of Great Britain, and
of her continental foes. Portraits of empire-builders hung on the wall, and
he pointed to them. He quoted imperial poets. He showed how patriotism
has broadened since the days of Shakespeare, who, for all his genuis, could
only write of his country as –
This fortress built by nature for herself
Against infection and the hand of war,
This happy breed of men, this little world,
This precious stone set in the silver sea.
And it seemed that only a short ladder lay between the preparation room and
the Anglo-Saxon hegemony of the globe. Then he paused, and in the silence
came 'sob, sob, sob,' from a little boy, who was regretting a villa in Guildford
and his mother's half acre of garden. (181–2)

Lending himself to this 'beneficent machine', Rickie soon
compromises his independence. Hardly aware of what he is
doing, he helps Herbert victimize a weak boy named Varden,
and before he knows it, he has become an administrative
puppet. As for Stephen, he puts him out of his mind, or at
least out of his conscious mind. He becomes wrapped in a
'cloud of unreality'. Agnes, who is her brother's agent more
than her husband's wife and is not without a sadistic streak,

jokingly asks Rickie, 'How is the cow today?' (203) But the answer, of course, is that the cow is no longer 'there'.

Rickie, however, cannot be left swaddled in his cloud forever. Like Lucy Honeychurch and Philip Herriton, he must be offered the chance to face the truth and thereby be saved. Stephen, accordingly, must be brought back into the action; and this Forster manages to do, first by the clumsy expedient of having the weak boy Varden mistake Stephen, whom he has never met, for somebody else and write him a letter, to which Stephen replies; and then, more plausibly, by having Agnes, who wants to inherit Aunt Emily's money, report to her that Stephen had once ridiculed her in front of Rickie (which he had) by reciting a rude poem about her. The upshot is that Aunt Emily, who has found Stephen a difficult ward anyway, expels him from Cadover, but gives him before he leaves a packet of papers describing his parentage and his relationship to Rickie. He finds his way to Sawston – 'A man, if he has a brother, may reasonably visit him' (248) – and the event precipitates Rickie's release from the bondage of school and a deteriorated marriage. Ansell, who has met Stephen in the garden of Dunwood House and read the packet, once again assumes the cloak of guide and soothsayer to reveal, implausibly but dramatically, to the entire school the fact that Stephen is the son not of Rickie's father but of his mother; and once again, Rickie faints.

In the novel's shortest chapter, which follows immediately, Forster underlines the nature of Rickie's failure. Having made his mother a symbol of absolute good, he now finds his soul 'bankrupt'. What then should he do? He might instead worship God, for God's image at least is 'incorruptible'. But to do so would be to deprive himself of more human satisfactions. A singleminded devotion to the Absolute

cannot give us friends, or the embrace of a lover, or the touch of children, for with our fellow-mortals it has no concern. It cannot even give the joys we call trivial – fine weather, the pleasures of meat and drink, bathing and the hot sand afterwards, running, dreamless sleep. Have we learnt the true discipline of a bankruptcy if we turn to such coinage as this? Will it really profit us so much if we save our souls and lose the whole world? (260)

Forster's final question poses the dilemma that confronts Rickie throughout his adult life and which his longest journey is an attempt to resolve – the choice between the transcendent and the mundane, the symbol and the reality, the absolute and the human. What is the value of personal 'salvation', Forster is asking, if we lose our humanity in order to gain it?

But Rickie, recovering from the shock of Ansell's disclosure, attempts both to show his humanity and be saved. This time he will not reject the symbolic moment. He will accept Stephen as his brother.

And so the final stage of his journey begins – the stage in which, responding to Stephen's invitation to come with him, he plunges into the 'impalpable cloud' (291) that engulfs Sawston and tries to make his way back to 'the Earth'. For to accept Stephen is to overrule the conventions that have thus far governed his attitude toward him and get back to 'the Earth' whose spirit Stephen embodies. Only the Earth, as he declares to his aunt on the day of his death, will 'confirm' him; only the Earth, that is, will strengthen his spirit and validate his life.

Rickie's desire to accept Stephen is realistic. The trouble is he accepts him in the wrong way. An incurable symboliser, he now sees him not as a symbol of his father's sin but of his mother's virtue. He cannot simply accept him as a human being with a life of his own. Hence, when he plunges into the fog in response to Stephen's call ('Come, I do mean it. Come...'), it is their mother's voice that he hears. 'Habits and sex may change with the new generation, features may alter with the play of a private passion, but a voice is apart from these. It lies nearer to the racial essence and perhaps to the divine; it can, at all events, overleap one grave.' (292)

The final chapters of the novel, then – all but the last – are chiefly concerned with Rickie's noble but misguided effort to accept Stephen and what he conceives to be the Earth. But the Earth for Rickie is not simply a natural realm with which man might achieve an organic relationship; it is a life-giving spirit, the goddess Demeter, whose portrait hangs from the ceiling in Stephen's room at Cadover.

He [Rickie] longed to be back riding over those windy fields, to be back in those mystic circles, beneath pure sky. Then they could have watched and helped and taught each other, until the word was a reality, and the past not a torn photograph, but Demeter the goddess rejoicing in the spring. Ah, if he had seized those high opportunities! For they led to the highest of all, the symbolic moment, which, if a man accepts, he has accepted life. (289)

Just as earlier, when praying to his mother, Rickie had raised his eyes above the 'mean houses' of Sawston to see in the night sky 'the frosty glories of Orion' (223), so now he turns his eyes earthward to see the joyful goddess Demeter. But Orion, symbolizing celestial transcendence and death, and Demeter, symbolizing nature's solicitude for life and growth, are equally remote from concrete reality. Orion's glories are 'frosty'. And as for nature, the novel points again and again to her utter indifference to human welfare. Rickie's lameness is as natural as Stephen's health, sudden death as natural as continuing life. It is natural that Rickie should live after Gerald dies, and that Stephen, not Rickie, should 'contribute to the stream' of life (222). The death of Rickie's daughter brings home to him 'the cruelty of Nature, to whom our refinement and piety are but as bubbles, hurrying downwards on the turbid waters' (221). But the lesson, once learnt, is apparently forgotten; for in the last days of his life, Rickie hopes for more from the Earth than she will give. One need only compare his romantic regard for 'Demeter' with Stephen's unimaginative love and acceptance of his surroundings to see the difference between their sensibilities. To Stephen, Rickie's mystical faith in getting in touch with Nature is 'cant' (140), for Stephen responds to the Earth like 'an animal with just enough soul to contemplate its own bliss' (243).

But Rickie cannot accept the Earth as it is; he must have his symbols and symbolic moments or nothing – and just before his death, he is left with nothing. Shattered by Stephen's drunkenness, he kneels, prays to God, and repudiates 'the Earth'. But 'the Earth', of course, is no more to be trusted than any of Rickie's other symbols. Accordingly, he repudiates all of the moments and values that he had considered supreme.

...the woman he loved would die out, in drunkenness, in debauchery, and her strength would be dissipated by a man, her beauty defiled in a man. She would not continue. That mystic rose and the face it illumined meant nothing. The stream – he was above it now – meant nothing, though it burst from the pure turf and ran for ever to the sea. The bather, the shoulders of Orion – they all meant nothing, and were going nowhere. The whole affair was a ridiculous dream. (319)

As he kneels, Orion rises behind him. Praying as Rickie does to God while at the same time repudiating his symbols, he has reached a state of 'spiritual muddledom' not unlike Mrs Moore's in *A Passage to India* – a state in which 'we can neither act nor refrain from action, we can neither ignore nor respect Infinity'.[3] And so when Stephen drunkenly falls across the tracks, Rickie 'wearily' does 'a man's duty' and pushes him to safety. But the oncoming train runs over Rickie's knees, a fatal injury ironically recalling 'the shattered knees' (325) of the Cnidian Demeter.

Rickie, then, the visionary idealist, sacrifices his life that Stephen, a youth chiefly guided by instinct and feeling, might live. The final chapter shows Stephen married and with a child, and leading the 'happy tangible life' of a country farmer a few miles from Cadover. Aunt Emily has died and bequeathed Cadover to the Silts, poor cousins of Rickie's father, who are making needed improvements in the property. Stephen and Herbert are busily preparing an edition of Rickie's stories, which have already enjoyed a moderate success; and at the beginning of the chapter they argue over the division of the profits. Ansell, however improbably, is living with Stephen and his family – a symbolic reminder that each in himself is incomplete. Stephen, for all his easy acceptance of himself and the Earth and his essential kindness, needs culture and wisdom. Ansell, on the other hand, needs something of Stephen's earthiness and passion.

[3] *A Passage to India*, 208. Harcourt, Brace, New York, 1952.

But why, the novel asks in conclusion, should Stephen live and Rickie die? 'By whose authority?' (326) And this, the ultimate question, is unanswerable. The 'deep truth', as Shelley said, is 'imageless'. In Stephen, however, and his descendants seems to lie – Forster suggests – England's best hope for the future. 'Though he could not phrase it, he believed that he guided the future of our race, and that, century after century, his thoughts and his passions would triumph in England. The dead who had evoked him, the unborn whom he would evoke – he governed the paths between them.' (326) And in line with this belief – or hope – the novel ends as Stephen, taking his child to sleep outdoors with him, muses on Rickie's fate and his own future.

He filled his pipe, and then sat pressing the unlit tobacco with his thumb. 'What am I to do?' he thought. 'Can he notice the things he gave me? A parson would know. But what's a man like me to do, who works all his life out of doors?' As he wondered, the silence of the night was broken. The whistle of Mr Pembroke's train came faintly, and a lurid spot passed over the land – passed, and the silence returned. One thing remained that a man of his sort might do. He bent down reverently and saluted the child; to whom he had given the name of their mother. (327)

The Longest Journey is carefully planned. As K. W. Gransden has pointed out,[4] its three major sections are like three parts of a symphony, the first part corresponding to the statement, the second part to the crisis, and the third part to the resolution. The musical analogy can be carried further. As in his other novels, Forster employs numerous 'echoes' or 'Leitmotifs' to relate different elements of the story. The imagery of streams and rivers, for example, recurs in various contexts to suggest nature and natural forces, whether beneficent or hostile to man. The chalk, which is so much a part of the Wiltshire soil, also occurs in the dell at Madingley, a fact that helps to connect the two regions with Rickie's sense of the Earth. Stephen intentionally smashes Aunt Emily's drawing-room window with a lump of chalk, and on the night of his death, Rickie accidentally drops the same lump on her teacup and breaks it. Thus the chalk, a part of the Earth, is dramati-

4 Gransden, p. 48.

cally opposed to his aunt's puerile conventionalism and to the 'teacup of experience', which we must drink or die (75). Refusing to drink it any longer, Rickie goes out of the house – to die. Among the objects whose significance cannot be grasped until the novel has been read through is the picture of Stockholm that hangs on the wall of Rickie's room in Cambridge (17). It had belonged to Rickie's mother, who had eloped to Stockholm with her lover Robert, who was drowned while swimming in the sea near there. The picture, which after Rickie's death hangs in Herbert's house, goes finally to Stephen. Another significant picture is the portrait of Demeter that hangs in Stephen's room in Cadover. It is 'echoed' in the famous statue of the Cnidian Demeter in the British Museum, which Ansell pauses to admire after leaving the Reading Room. Ansell's mandala is recalled in the architecture of the Reading Room with its 'radiating desks, and the central area, where the catalogue shelves curve round the superintendent's throne' (204). Here Ansell spends his hours 'seeking for truth though truth is unattainable'. And when Rickie looks forward to the birth of his child, Forster again invokes the mandala to suggest the reality that Rickie hopes to find in the event.

In the midst of lessons he would grow dreamy, as one who spies a new symbol for the universe, a fresh circle within the square. Within the square shall be a circle, within the circle another square, until the visual eye is baffled. Here is meaning of a kind. His mother had forgotten herself in him. He would forget himself in his son. (211)

Ever sensitive to music, Forster has carefully deployed his echoes in a way that looks back to Wagner and forward to Proust.

Yet despite its searching exploration of theme and careful planning, *The Longest Journey* is the least popular of Forster's novels as it is also in some respects the least successful. Certainly a major bar to the novel's popularity is Rickie himself, who to many readers must seem, as he does to Stephen, an 'anaemic prig'. How can one empathize with a man who actually faints at the news that he has a bastard brother? And certainly the very issue of bastardy dates the novel. A more up-to-date analogue of Rickie's effort to accept Stephen would be that of an average white American suddenly stunned with the news that he had just acquired a black son-in-law. Would he find him easier to accept than Rickie finds Stephen? Would he be less likely to turn him into a symbol?

The Longest Journey is also overladen with incidents that add little or nothing to its development of the central theme. As Lionel Trilling has said, there is 'too-much steam that blows up the boiler'.[5] There are too many details relating to Aunt Emily's mismanagement of her estate, too many specimens of her late husband's aphorisms. Stephen's ride with the soldier and its aftermath are recounted at too great a length. In an early draft of the novel, this episode was even longer (see Forster's Introduction to the World's Classics edition). Rickie's mother's affair with Robert seems needlessly detailed. One may also question whether Forster's satire of public school life, effective though it is as satire, does not weaken the novel as a whole. Had Sawston School been depicted as less patently bad, had Rickie been allowed to teach at a reasonably good school, he would have had to discriminate more carefully among the 'realities' to which he was exposed.

That Forster chose, however, to confront Rickie with a bad school points to what seems to me the novel's greatest flaw, its confusion of aims. It tries to be both realistic and allegorical, and the two aims do not harmonize. Forster in fact betrays the same fault as Rickie: he treats some of the characters as symbols while insisting upon their reality. Stephen, for instance, regarded as a human being, must be one of the least plausible yokels in literature since Wordsworth's *Lyrical Ballads*. His speech is wooden ('Here am I, Rickie, and there are you, a fair wreck.' (291)) and his actions are often more determined by his symbolic role than by psychological plausibility. His fight and reconciliation with Ansell is a case in point. His drunken return to Dunwood House and invitation to Rickie to leave his wife and join him is another. Most of the time, Stephen behaves like a symbol, and not a very compelling one;

[5] Lionel Trilling, *E. M. Forster*, p. 76. Norfolk, Conn., 1943.

yet Rickie is asked to accept him as a man, and so, by implication, is the reader.

Forster's treatment of Herbert Pembroke also displays a
'double vision'. On the one hand, he tries to regard him as
a mixture of good and bad, a rounded human being; on the
other, he sees him as a fool, a hypocrite, and a swindler. One
need only compare the following description of Herbert with
his actual conduct to see that something indeed is 'amiss':

What was amiss with Herbert?...The man was kind and unselfish; more than
that, he was truly charitable, and it was a real pleasure to him to give pleasure
to others. Certainly he might talk too much about it afterwards; but it was
the doing, not the talking, that he really valued, and benefactors of this sort
are not too common. He was, moreover, diligent and and conscientious: his
heart was in his work, and his adherence to the Church of England no mere
matter of form. He was capable of affection: he was usually courteous and
tolerant. Then what was amiss? Why, in spite of all these qualities, should
Rickie feel that there was something wrong with him – nay, that he was wrong
as a whole, and that if the Spirit of Humanity should ever hold a judgment
he would assuredly be classed among the goats? The answer at first sight
appeared a graceless one – it was that Herbert was stupid. Not stupid in the
ordinary sense – he had a business-like brain, and acquired knowledge easily
– but stupid in the important sense: his whole life was coloured by a contempt
of the intellect. (190–1)

Yet this is the man who, after vainly trying to marry a woman
solely for his own political gain, persecutes her ward Varden,
and tries to cheat Stephen out of his rightful share of the
profits from the sale of Rickie's stories. This is the man of
whom, by the end of the novel, Forster can say,

To him all criticism was 'rudeness': he never heeded it, for he never needed
it: he was never wrong. All his life he had ordered little human beings about,
and now he was equally magisterial to big ones: Stephen was a fifth-form lout
whom, owing to some flaw in the regulations, he could not send up to the
headmaster to be caned. (324)

Forster's antipathy to Herbert's values clashed with his sense
of psychological realism, with the result that he created not
a character but a caricature, as symbolic of the bad life as
Stephen is of the good.

Agnes is a more complicated figure than Herbert, yet she

too is unconvincing. She is a bundle of characteristics (health, kindness, aggressiveness, sadism, materialism, cunning) that never fuses into a character, for Forster's view of her is mainly external and in relation to Rickie. Consequently, his plea that she too 'has her tragedy' (229) rings hollow. Of course a bad marriage is generally 'tragic' for both parties; but we cannot feel the force of her suffering since it is never revealed.

Rickie's father and mother are also unconvincing, for Forster sees them as Rickie does. They are soap-opera figures, the father urbane, cultivated and cold; the mother insipidly sweet – 'beautiful without and within' (33).

Forster's close identification with Rickie also at times betrays him into sentimentality and ambiguity. What, for example, is his attitude to Rickie's feelings when Rickie sees Agnes and Gerald kissing? While it may be true, as J. B. Beer has suggested,[6] that the tone of this much criticized 'purple passage' is meant to reflect Rickie's adolescent romanticism, it is hard not to feel that when Forster writes such phrases as 'The riot of fair images...invaded his being and lit lamps at unsuspecting shrines...He stood at the springs of creation', he is participating in Rickie's mood. Similarly, Rickie's sentimental lament for a vanished past – 'Ah, if he had seized those high opportunities!' (289) – is pretty clearly Forster's too. Or consider the ambiguity of the following passage in which Forster 'bounces' the reader between Rickie's point of view and his own, and muddles the two together:

In Cadover, the perilous house, Agnes had already parted from Mrs Failing. His thoughts returned to her. Was she, the soul of truth, in safety? Was her purity vexed by the lies and selfishness? Would she elude the caprice which had, he vaguely knew, caused suffering before? Ah, the frailty of joy! Ah, the myriads of longings that pass without fruition, and the turf grows over them! Better men, women as noble – they had died up here and their dust had been mingled, but only their dust. These are morbid thoughts, but who dare contradict them? There is much good luck in the world, but it is luck. We are none of us safe. We are children, playing or quarrelling on the line, and some of us have Rickie's temperament, or his experiences, and admit it. So he mused...(129)

6   J. B. Beer, The Achievement of E. M. Forster, pp. 86–8. London, 1963.

46

The first two sentences establish the situation. The next two express Rickie's musings; so, too, does the third, except for the qualifying phrase 'he vaguely knew', by which Forster distinguishes between Rickie's vague awareness and his own precise knowledge. In the next three sentences – 'Ah, the fraility...but only their dust' – Forster and Rickie appear to join forces in a banal and rather incoherent lament over the vicissitudes of life. The next four sentences – 'These are morbid thoughts...and admit it' – express Forster's views; though in the fourth, he clearly identifies his temperament and experience with Rickie's. Finally, 'So he mused...' suggests either that all of the foregoing passage or an indeterminate part of it represents Rickie's thoughts. Such writing is one source of the incoherence in the novel about which critics have complained.

Nevertheless, with all of its manifest weaknesses, *The Longest Journey* is uniquely important to an understanding of Forster's mind and his aspirations as a novelist. Rickie's search for 'reality' is also his author's. Like Rickie, Forster is divided in his loyalties – divided between the inner life and the outer, between what Keats called 'the holiness of the heart's affections and the truth of imagination' on the one hand, and the human world in all its rich complexity on the other. More intimately than Forster's other novels, *The Longest Journey* presents his desire to bridge the world of spirit and objective fact.

3

The Short Stories

I

Like his novels, most of Forster's short stories[1] turn on the exposure of one or more characters, generally through travel, to a new order of experience. A group of English tourists encounters in Italy the great god Pan; an elderly Englishman experiences an 'eternal moment' in a grove of plane trees in Greece; a small boy goes to Heaven in a celestial omnibus; a Roman youth, conducting his sister on a difficult journey, is raped by a Goth in the woods; an army captain en route to India has a disastrous affair with a half-caste native; and so on. Some of the travellers are revitalized by their encounters; some are frightened; some destroyed. But whatever the final result, their outlook is likely to be transformed.

The best of the stories convey searching and subtle insights into the human condition, a few are quite weighty; but, typically, they are light, whimsical and ironic, their comedy partly arising from Forster's carefully controlled tone and point of view, partly from the contrast between the travellers' naive expectations and their actual experiences.

Most of the stories that comprise the *Collected Tales*, Forster declares, are fantasies. They deal with the imaginary and supernatural, taking the traveller from the tangible, everyday world to an impalpable and mysterious one, embodying the power of the unseen.

In 'The Story of a Panic' – one of the best of the fantasies – a party of English tourists go for a picnic to a secluded valley

[1] Contained in the *Collected Tales* (1947) and the posthumously published *The Life to Come and Other Stories* (1972). With one exception, the twelve stories in the earlier volume were published before the First World War. The thirteen stories in the second volume were written between 1903 and 1958, but only one of them, 'Albergo Empedocle', had previously appeared in print.

near Ravello and there encounter the spirit of Pan. The great god, long presumed dead, appears as a mysterious 'catspaw of wind', which strikes panic into the hearts of the adults, who flee at its approach. Only Eustace, a repressed and moody boy of fourteen, is exhilarated by the encounter; and he in fact is permanently transformed. That night he escapes from his hotel bedroom into the courtyard below, where, to the astonishment of Mr Tytler, the complacent and snobbish narrator, and the other awakened adults, he proceeds grandiloquently to expatiate on 'the great forces and manifestations of Nature' (28).[2] He is returned to his room; but later, with the help of Gennaro, a sympathetic young waiter, he escapes again. Together they leap from a second-floor window into the courtyard. The fall kills Gennaro, but Eustace, uninjured, climbs over the garden wall, swings down from an olive tree, and escapes, presumably forever. 'Signora Safetti [the landlady] burst into screams at the sight of the dead body, and, far down the valley towards the sea, there still resounded the shouts and the laughter of the escaping boy.' (38)

The story's considerable impact stems in great measure from Forster's care in delineating the setting and characters. Like several other epiphanous spots in his fiction (for example, the dell at Madingley, the Cadbury Rings, the Marabar Caves, the grove of plane trees at Plataniste), the valley where 'Pan' appears is cut off from the rest of the world and seems to possess a peculiarly retentive power. As Mr Tytler describes it, it is both beautiful and sinister:

The valley ended in a vast hollow, shaped like a cup, into which radiated ravines from the precipitous hills around. Both the valley and the ravines and the ribs of hill that divided the ravines were covered with leafy chestnut, so that the general appearance was that of a many-fingered green hand, palm upwards, which was clutching convulsively to keep us in its grasp. Far down the valley we could see Ravello and the sea, but that was the only sign of another world. (5-6)

The adults who choose this site for their picnic are well contrasted; but they have one thing in common, they are ill

2 All page references in *Collected Tales* are from the Knopf, 1952 edition.

attuned to the unseen. Besides Tytler, the most notable are Mr Leyland, a would-be artist and sentimental aesthete, and Mr Sandbach, a pontifical clergyman who has undertaken to tutor Eustace. Principally through these three characters, Forster cleverly prepares for the first of the story's two climaxes. As they admire the scenery, Leyland laments that 'All the poetry is going from Nature...her lakes and marshes are drained, her seas banked up, her forests cut down. Everywhere we see the vulgarity of desolation spreading.' (8) Taking a more practical and economic view, Tytler defends the cutting of trees and the right of landlords to make money from their land. But the woods, Leyland reminds everyone, 'no longer give shelter to Pan'; and when Mr Sandbach remarks that that is because 'Pan is dead . . . The great God Pan is dead', Leyland abandons himself 'to that mock misery in which artistic people are so fond of indulging' (9). Pan to Leyland, of course, is the benevolent guardian of sheep – 'Pan ovium custos' – not the sinister deity equally known to literature and mythology. The nature that all of the adults admire is Arcadian. Consequently, they are unprepared for the 'catspaw of wind' that races mysteriously up the ridge on which they are standing. Their inability to cope with the wind signifies a spiritual failure. They cannot cope with it because, as representative adults, they have repressed their emotional and instinctive drives. The wind, which is unexpected and inexplicable, corresponds to their repressed unconscious, to what Jung calls the shadow. 'If we step through the door of the shadow,' he writes, 'we discover with terror that we are the objects of unseen factors. To know this is decidedly unpleasant. . . It can even give rise to primitive panic.'[3] Only Eustace, who, as a boy, still communes with his 'shadow,' is exhilarated by the encounter, and is drawn to worship 'Pan' as an all embracing power. Only he appears to be saved from the emotionally inhibiting forces of adult life.

But how saved is Eustace? Not, one suspects, completely. Certainly it is a salvation unlikely to win much sympathy from

[3] C. G. Jung, *The Archetypes and the Collective Unconscious*: Collected Works, vol. 9, part 1, 2nd edn, p. 23. Princeton, 1969.

the average reader, for Eustace remains to the end an unap-
pealing boy, moody, selfish, and secretive. His attachment to
Gennaro might on the surface seem redeeming; Gennaro too
is a 'natural' and as much of a misfit as a waiter as Eustace
seems to be as a boy; but that Eustace's feeling for him is too
self-seeking to be called love is underlined by the waiter's death
and the boy's carefree escape from all human concern and
responsibility. Eustace's natural piety, in fact, cannot embrace
the human, as he himself declares when, praising the great
forces and manifestations of nature, he adds, 'and then there
are men, but I can't make them out so well'. Accordingly, he
escapes from humanity; but in Forster's ethic, a salvation that
evades the human is an ambiguous one at best.

Salvation is more straightforward in the next two stories,
'The Other Side of the Hedge' and 'The Celestial Omnibus'.
The first is little more than a fable. The hedge divides the
winding, dusty road of life down which mankind is hurrying
to who knows where, from the earthly paradise. After crawling
exhausted through a gap in the hedge and being rescued from
drowning in the surrounding moat, the narrator finds himself
in a pastoral country whose inhabitants, as he learns from his
rescuer and guide, are unprogressive and agricultural. Lovely
as it all is, the traveller feels that nevertheless he might like
to rejoin the rat race, for, after all, as his pedometer has told
him, he is only twenty-five. But, after a bit more sight-seeing,
he is tired and thirsty – so thirsty that he steals a can of beer
from a passer-by. Drinking, he sinks into oblivion, but discovers just before doing so that the man whose beer he has
taken and who is now lowering him gently to sleep off its
effects is his long-forsaken brother. Unlike Eustace who
escaped from humanity, the present traveller escapes to it.
Love and friendship, the story suggests, flourish best under
elemental conditions.

In 'The Celestial Omnibus', the boy escapes from a dreary
suburb and a couple of dreary parents to heaven. The suburb
is gray and monotonous; the parents are facetious and superficial; their friend Mr Bons is a pompous fraud – a literateur

who collects books ('I believe we have seven Shelleys') as some people collect art, and who patronises the boy. But the boy, just because he is a boy, is nearer the celestial light than his elders. Hence he ascends to heaven – not, however, on the wings of poesy but in a horse-drawn celestial omnibus piloted, on three separate occasions, by Sir Thomas Browne, Jane Austen, and Dante. And the heaven to which he goes, together with Mr Bons, is a romantic fantasy of heights and depths, swirling clouds, Rhine Maidens, heroes, and eminent authors. The boy remains in heaven, but Mr Bons, who quotes poetry without having proved it upon his pulses, crashes down to a horrible death. Entertaining as it is, the story is encumbered with incident and saved from sentimentality only by Forster's wit and lightness of touch.

'Other Kingdom' is another escapist fantasy, but a better one. The conflict between Harcourt Worters and Evelyn Beaumont, his fiancée, who runs away from him and turns into a tree, is treated in a spirit of Meridithean comedy. The situation in fact recalls *The Egoist.* Like Sir Willoughby Patterne, Harcourt is handsome, virile, and rich, and lives in a big country house surrounded by a worshipful family, including his mother, two maiden sisters (Sir Willoughby has two maiden aunts), an impecunious young ward Jack Ford (compare Crossjay Patterne), his ward's Latin tutor Mr Inskip (compare Vernon Whitford), and a retinue of servants. A successful and not overscrupulous businessman, Harcourt resembles Sir Willoughby in his egoism. He can enjoy only what he possesses, and like Sir Willoughby he wants to possess his wife. Evelyn Beaumont is as unsuited to be married to such a man as Clara Middleton was to Sir Willoughby. In fact, she recalls Meredith's heroine in temperament and circumstance, for she is gay and impulsive, a psychologically free spirit whose inexperience and naivety have engaged her to the wrong kind of man.

Their story is told by Mr Inskip, whose sycophantic regard for Harcourt, appreciation for classical myth and literature, and failure to understand the crucial events to which he contributes enhances the irony. Sensitive and self-deceiving, he can communicate the superior values of the 'other kingdom' while subscribing, out of material self-regard, to the inferior ones of this. He can enjoy Evelyn's impulsive gaiety and admire Ford's idealism, yet Harcourt is his man; for a Latin teacher without independent means must, as Jane Austen might have said, be in need of a rich employer.

The crisis is broached by Harcourt's purchase of Other Kingdom, an adjacent copse, as a wedding present for Evelyn. True to his nature, Harcourt wants to fence it off from the outside world and build an asphalt path between it and his house. But Evelyn will not hear of a fence or path. 'I don't want to be fenced in...I hate fences. And bridges. And all paths.' (96) Furthermore, she values just what Harcourt cannot abide – the fact that the boys and girls of the village have for ages come to Other Kingdom and cut their initials in the trees.

They cut their names and go away, and when the first child is born they come again and deepen the cuts. So for each child. That's how you know: the initials that go right through to the wood are the fathers and mothers of large families, and the scratches in the bark that soon close up are boys and girls who were never married at all. (95–6)

In her wish to preserve the copse in its natural state, Evelyn obviously speaks for Forster. The passage looks forward to similar ones in *Howards End* commemorating the life of tradition as nurtured by the country and the folklore associated with the wych-elm. Evelyn's feeling, too, that the outside world should not be excluded from Other Kingdom is in keeping with Forster's visionary humanism. On the one hand, there is an ideal realm, harmonious and self-contained, as projected in vision and realized in art; on the other, there is humanity and the world of daily life with which the novelist and humanist must concern himself. Forster's belief in art for art's sake because it 'creates little worlds of its own' testifies to his sympathy with what is beyond the human; whereas his fiction and social criticism amply testify to his concern with humanity. Just so, in *The Longest Journey*, Rickie Elliot, the character who most intimately speaks for Forster, realizes that, for all its beauty and seclusion, the dell at Madingley must be available to all. 'He did not love the vulgar herd, but he knew that his own vulgarity would be greater if he forbade it ingress, and that it was not by preciosity that he would attain to the intimate spirit of the dell.' It is Harcourt, then, intent like Sir Willoughby in keeping the outer world without, who is vulgar; and Evelyn, willing to admit others into her kingdom, who possesses the aristocracy of spirit that he can only ape.

Their conflict comes to a head when Harcourt gets hold of Ford's 'practically private notebook', reads in it the latter's love poems to Evelyn, and perhaps sees the picture of himself blushing 'like a boiled lobster'. For this piece of treachery Ford must be expelled. Evelyn, after all, is his, Harcourt's, property – 'My haven from the world! My temple of purity.' Evelyn, for her part, cannot believe that Harcourt would be so ungenerous, but, finding that he is, finally manages her escape, though not before Harcourt has had his way with Other Kingdom. 'The bridge is built, the fence finished, and Other Kingdom lies tethered by a ribbon of asphalt to our front door.' The climactic scene, with Evelyn running toward Other Kingdom and Harcourt hot in pursuit, parodies the legend of Daphne and Apollo (although the tempest that precedes and follows Evelyn's disappearance may have been borrowed from *The Egoist*: Clara Middleton flees during a thunderstorm). Evelyn's feeling for myth and folklore, as expressed in the Latin lesson that begins the story and in her reference to the initials that the boys and girls have cut in the beech barks, has prepared us for her role. Her transformation has also been foreshadowed when, in playful appreciation of Harcourt's purchase, she tries to imitate a beech. 'She flung her arms up above her head...like the layers of a beech.' Now as she flees, Evelyn assumes mythic dimensions. She represents freedom and nature, the antithesis to Harcourt's sham world with its machinery of servants, fences, and asphalt paths, and its pretension to claims, position, and rights.

She danced to the song of a bird that sang passionately in Other Kingdom, and the river held back its waves to watch her (one might have supposed), and the winds lay spellbound in their cavern, and the great clouds spellbound in the sky. She danced away from our society and our life, back, back, through the centuries till houses and fences fell and the earth lay wild to the sun. Her garment was as foliage upon her, the strength of her limbs as boughs, her throat the smooth upper branch that salutes the morning or glistens to the rain. Leaves move, leaves hide it as hers was hidden by the motion of her hair. Leaves move again and it is ours, as her throat was ours again when, parting the tangle, she faced us crying, 'Oh!' crying, 'Oh Harcourt! I never was so happy. I have all that there is in the world.' (108–9)

Her only human rapport is with Ford; for the youth, in his quietly enigmatic way, has stood for the simple and natural.

He cannot understand the footman and the solid silver kettle-stand. They make him cross. For he had dreams – not exactly spiritual dreams: Mr Worters is the man for those – but dreams of the tangible and the actual: robust dreams, which take him, not to heaven, but to another earth. There are no footmen in this other earth, and the kettle-stands, I suppose, will not be made of silver, and I know that everything is to be itself, and not practically something else. (83–4)

Studious, clear-sighted, witty, rather detached yet able to love, Ford is temperamentally closer to Forster than to Crossjay Patterne, his counterpart in *The Egoist*. With the notebook in which he writes, he is an artist-figure, and it is due to him and his poetry that Evelyn escapes. Supported, in other words, though he is by a tasteless materialism, he is the means through which the visionary ideal is realized. And the vision repays the debt. Just as he had once, during the picnic at Other Kingdom, blocked Evelyn's view of Harcourt's ugly house, so now she will screen Ford from the withering character of Harcourt's influence. 'Oh Ford! oh Ford, among all these Worters, I am coming through you to my Kingdom. Oh Ford, my lover while I was a woman, I will never forget you, never, as long as I have branches to shade you from the sun.' (109) The story ends with Ford in exile in a 'squalid suburb', ironically engrossed, when Harcourt and Inskip enter his room in pursuit of Evelyn, in the 'Oedipus Coloneus' of Sophocles. Solitary and self-contained, he sees what Harcourt can never see, that the free spirit cannot be fenced and possessed as Harcourt possesses his property. 'She has escaped you absolutely, for ever and

ever, as long as there are branches to shade men from the sun.'
(112)

'Other Kingdom' is one of Forster's best stories. Carefully
and dramatically structured, it is a sustained comedy gen-
erated by the confrontation of opposites: the civilized and the
natural, the sham and the true, the ugly and the beautiful, the
dead and the vital. If, finally, it is clever and entertaining
rather than profound, it is because it primarily deals with
manners and conduct rather than with the attitudes and
impulses that help to guide them.

'The Curate's Friend' is a much slighter tale. Yet it has an
amusing twist. It shows how a not-too-humble curate is led by
a spiritual encounter to worldly success. The curate is a callow
and histrionic youth who one day, while picnicking with his
fiancée, her mother, and another young man, encounters a
faun. The creature offers to make him wealthy; but, scorning
the offer, the curate tells him to make others happy instead.
'On this very hill sits a young lady for whom I have a high
regard. Commence with her. Aha! your face falls. I thought
as much. *You cannot do anything.* Here is the conclusion of the
whole matter!' (120) But the faun takes up the challenge, and
when the curate returns to the picnic spot, it is to find his
fiancée and the other young man locked in each other's arms.
Scornfully the curate dismisses them and then, in solitude,
faces the facts. 'I thought of my injured pride, of my baffled
unselfishness, of Emily, whom I was losing through no fault
of her own, of the little friend, who just then slipped beneath
the heavy tea basket, and that decided me, and I laughed.' (123)
No more wanting to marry Emily, as he now realizes, than she
him, he settles into a bachelor's life and becomes a happy,
worldly, and respected curate. His encounter with pagan
nature has helped him to contribute to the happiness of his
Christian parishioners, who in turn reward him materially and
spiritually. But he dare not tell them the source of his joy, 'for
if I breathed one word of that, my present life, so agreeable
and profitable, would come to an end, my congregation would
depart, and so should I, and instead of being an asset to

my parish, I might find myself an expense to the nation' (124).

The connection implied between spiritual enlightenment and material success may seem oddly un-Forsterian; but it is not. Forster's spiritually enlightened characters are seldom hard-up, and three of them, Miss Raby, Margaret Schlegel, and Mrs Wilcox, are conspicuously well-off. Like Shaw and Butler, Forster seems to feel that money and comfort are highly desirable spiritual props.

The title of Forster's next story, 'The Road from Colonus', – and it is one of his two best – ironically recalls Sophocles' great play. Forster's 'Oedipus' is an aging, querulous Englishman, Mr Lucas, who, accompanied by his daughter Ethel, a young Mr Graham, and a Mrs Forman, is fulfilling a lifetime wish to visit Greece. But it is not until Mr Lucas visits an out-of-the-way settlement mainly consisting of a Khan (inn) and a grove of plane trees that he sees 'the real Greece'. Up to this point the country had proved disappointing. 'Athens had been dusty, Delphi wet, Thermopylae flat, and he had listened with amazement and cynicism to the rapturous exclamations of his companions.' (127) Plataniste, however, enchants him. Though the surrounding country is hot and dry, here there is shade, and even a stream, which issues mysteriously from the hollowed-out trunk of a plane tree in which the local inhabitants have hung votive offerings. Mr Lucas, who has ridden ahead of his companions ('he was perhaps reaching the age at which independence becomes valuable, because it is so soon to be lost'), enters the tree trunk and allows the water, which wells up from subterraneous depths, to bathe his ankles. And for him at this point, the world of time is invaded by eternity. 'His eyes closed, and he had the strange feeling of one who is moving, yet at peace – the feeling of the swimmer, who, after long struggling with chopping seas, finds that after all the tide will sweep him to his goal. So he lay motionless, conscious only of the stream below his feet, and that all things were a stream, in which he was moving.' Opening his eyes, he sees for the first time a coherent world in which all things have meaning.

There was meaning in the stoop of the old woman over her work, and in the quick motions of the little pig, and in her diminishing globe of wool. A young man came singing over the streams on a mule, and there was beauty in his pose and sincerity in his greeting. The sun made no accidental patterns upon the spreading roots of the trees, and there was intention in the nodding clumps of asphodel, and in the music of the water. To Mr Lucas, who, in a brief space of time, had discovered not only Greece, but England and all the world and life, there seemed nothing ludicrous in the desire to hang within the tree another votive offering – a little model of an entire man. (130)

Mr Lucas's reverie is rudely shattered by the arrival of his companions, oo-ing and aah-ing with sentimental hyperbole over the beauty of the surroundings; to which Mr Lucas, rendered inexpressive by deep feeling, can only reply that the place 'impresses me very favourably' and other words to that effect. The place in fact impresses Mr Lucas so favourably that, like Oedipus at Colonus, he wants to stop there, at least for one night.

To sleep in the Khan with the gracious, kind-eyed country people, to watch the bats flit about within the globe of shade, and see the moon turn the golden patterns into silver – one such night would place him beyond relapse, and confirm him for ever in the kingdom he had regained. (132)

To humour him, his companions at first pretend that they would like nothing better; but it soon becomes apparent to Mr Lucas that they have no such intention. Where he has responded to the eternal, they know only the world of time. There are schedules to meet and places to get to. 'Enroute!' says the shrill voice of Mrs Forman. 'Ethel! Mr Graham! The best of things must come to an end.' (133) And so the place becomes a battleground with Mr Lucas, morally and physically supported by the inhabitants of the Khan, trying to stay, and his companions, by trickery and physical force, finally forcing him to leave.

The last part of the story finds Mr Lucas back in his London house with his daughter Ethel. Old and fretful he has nothing to look forward to but the arrival of his sister, whom he hates, to keep house for him. Everything upsets him – the street noises, the piano next door, and especially the sound of water gurgling through an overhead pipe. 'There's nothing I dislike more than running water.' The morning's mail brings a parcel from Mrs Forman in Greece – asphodel bulbs wrapped in a Greek newspaper. And one of the papers contains news of 'a rural disaster'. Ethel proceeds to read it aloud. A tree blew down at Plataniste, crushing to death the five occupants of the Khan. And from the date of the paper, the accident clearly happened the day that Mr Lucas and his companions left. Ethel's response to the news is the crowning irony. 'She was aghast at the narrowness of the escape, and for a long time kept silence. At last she said: "Such a marvellous deliverance does make one believe in Providence."' (143) But Mr Lucas is only concerned with the present. Without replying, he proceeds to compose a letter of complaint to his landlord.

The story's strength depends in part on the character of Mr Lucas. Touchy and self-centred, yet with a desire and potentiality for self-transcendence, he is both individual and archetypal. Forster's rendition of his 'eternal moment' is psychologically realistic. He gives us an inside view of it rather than an external, mythologized one as in 'The Story of a Panic' and 'Other Kingdom', and faces, too, its psychological implications. Intense and compelling as the moment is, it is also, we realize, only for one time and one place. Far from being able to 'transfigure the face of the world', it cannot even withstand the impact of everyday life – the arrival of Mrs Forman and the others, and the impress of London with its cacophony of sounds and endless series of petty irritants. Like Mrs Moore who, in *A Passage to India*, enjoys a similar moment of mystical rapture, Mr Lucas declines into apathy and inertia. He cannot connect the poetry of life with its prose, and finally the prose engulfs him. Eliot's 'Prufrock' might supply his epitaph: 'Till human voices wake us and we drown.'

As for the windstorm that destroys the Khan and all its inhabitants on the very day of Mr Lucas's visit, one may, I think, justly accuse Forster of indulging in a facile coincidence in order to end the story with an ironic punch. Nevertheless, the windstorm also underscores the temporal and psychological character of Mr Lucas's vision. The peace and harmony that he felt within the plane-tree grove was inspired by the character of the scene at that particular time. But nature can also be violent, destructive, chaotic. Order and meaning can collapse in an instant. Within the grove, Mr Lucas is, as it were, for perhaps the only time in his life, an artist, endowing with unity and meaning the diverse elements in the surrounding landscape. He is a surrogate for Forster who, as a novelist, strives to give form and meaning to the raw material of experience; for art, as Forster declares in 'Art for Art's Sake', is the only object in an essentially chaotic universe to possess internal order.[4] Hence the windstorm at Plataniste. Embodying the spirit of chaos, it is an implicit comment on the temporal and psychological character of Mr Lucas's vision, just as in *A Passage to India* the Marabar Caves afford a similar comment on Mrs Moore's erstwhile mystical sense of oneness with the universe. Visionary truth and objective reality, the story suggests, may be irreconcilable. Art is one thing, life another. Unable to connect the two elements of his experience, Mr Lucas loses the vision and succumbs to actuality. But Forster, a tougher, more gifted man, conveys through art his double commitment to vision and actuality and his desire to fuse them.

The next tale, 'The Machine Stops', is Forster's only piece of science fiction, a pre-Orwellian prophecy of things to come. Human beings are living in isolation in a subterranean hell. Each one lives in his separate compartment, his entire life governed by the Machine, his needs and wants limited to what the Machine can provide. Thanks to the marvels of the Machine, he can talk to others, listen to lectures and music, have all his physical needs catered for – all without leaving his cell. There are two characters, Vashti, an elderly woman with 'advanced' ideas, who is completely attuned to her environment, and Kuno her reactionary son, who is sufficiently maladjusted to his to escape by way of a ventilator shaft to the earth's surface (Wessex), which he enjoys for a few hours until he is recaptured by the horrible wormlike 'Mending

[4] *Two Cheers for Democracy*, 94–5. Harcourt, Brace, New York, 1951.

60

Apparatus' and returned to his cell. Kuno, who speaks for Forster, yearns for direct human contact: man to him, not the Machine, must be the measure of things. Vashti, on the other hand, prefers 'ideas' to direct experience, and is content to communicate through the Machine. She is one of Forster's unmaternal, detached women. The climax comes when the Machine breaks down. Chaos and Ancient Night reclaim the world, and everyone dies in the accompanying panic. But before death overtakes Kuno and Vashti, they enjoy a brief sympathetic reunion during which Kuno, who has seen human beings on the earth's surface, predicts that they will rebuild civilization without use of a Machine. 'Humanity has learnt its lesson.'

As a story 'The Machine Stops' is second-rate science fiction. It is too long and discursive, and its setting is more interesting than the characters. As a prognosis, however, it seems remarkably on target. If Forster had written the story in 1970 rather than sixty years ago, there would be few of its details that he might wish to change.

A more interesting story, though not a completely successful one, is 'The Point of It'. Michael, its protagonist, is an Edwardian liberal. He loves humanity and wants to serve it; he is tolerant, sympathetic, broad-minded, gentle. And because it was 'the moment in civilization for his type', he becomes a success, rising to a high post with the British Museum and earning a knighthood. But Michael's liberalism, the story suggests, is a tame substitute for his 'eternal moment'. That moment, with which the story begins, occurred in his youth when he was in a boat with his friend Harold and urged Harold to row with all his might. Since Harold had a weak heart and Michael was expected to help take care of him, the urging was injudicious. But 'the point of it' is that, as never again, Michael was joyously, spontaneously, alive. His mind and heart were united in common cause. Scene and action cohered in a magical unity.

He looked at the flaming windows and fancied that the farm was a star and the boat its attendant satellite. Then the tide was the rushing ether stream

61

of the universe, the interstellar surge that beats forever. How jolly! He did
not formulate his joys, after the weary fashion of older people. He was far
too happy to be thankful. (200)

But Michael's happiness leads to Harold's death. 'I – I don't
see the point of it', Michael had nervously exclaimed at the
sudden sense that his friend was overdoing it. 'Don't you?'
replies Harold. 'Well, you will some day.' But Harold dies 'half
in the boat and half out of it' before they can reach the shore.

The remainder of the story is taken up with Michael's later
life – and after-life. Comforting himself that he was after all
'worthier of life, and of whatever may come after it' than
Harold, having been born of 'a more intellectual stock', he
proceeds to cultivate his love of humanity (203). Janet, his wife,
has the starch that he lacks, for she is ruled by the head rather
than the heart, and unlike Michael prefers truth to tolerance.
Michael's mildness facilitates his professional advancement
but finally proves his undoing. Asked in his old age to adjudi-
cate a dispute among a group of women over a fish, Michael
replies 'that he had not sufficient data to judge on' and
advises them 'to lay the fish aside for twenty-four hours'. One
of the women,' the worse for drink', slaps him in the face with
the fish; he falls, and never recovers (210–11). On his deathbed,
he overhears his children condemn the mediocrity of his life;
and at that, 'the immense and superhuman cynicism that is
latent in all of us came at last to the top and transformed him.
He saw the abusurdity of love, and the vision so tickled him
that he began to laugh.' (213)

But his cynicism is insufficient to comfort him in the after-life.
After dying, he finds himself sunk in a vast sandy desert, which
is, as he learns, the 'heaven of the soft'. With him lie 'the
sentimentalists, the conciliators, the peace-makers, the hum-
anists, and all who have trusted the warmer vision' (218). Such
a hell perhaps implies the lack of a strong spiritual foundation
for modern liberalism. Compare Fielding's comment in *A
Passage to India*, 'We all build upon sand, and the more modern
the country gets, the worse'll be the crash.'[5] Michael's wife, who

[5] *A Passage to India*, 276. Harcourt, Brace, New York, 1952.

predeceased him, must surely, he feels, be in the 'heaven of the hard', a range of stony mountains that he can see in the distance. An eternity in either place would be hell indeed. But Michael, at any rate, is to be spared. He is spared not because of what he has done (for it is Forster's point that Michael's kind of liberalism cannot do much) but because of what he desires. Lying in the sand, he hears a voice 'inexpressibly sweet', the voice of the transcendent spirit that had once 'transfigured the world' and that still governs the years between childhood and maturity. It is the spirit that had possessed Michael when he was in the boat with Harold. Again he desires it, and since 'desire is enough', he is saved. Dying a second death, he finds himself once more being rowed in a boat in an estuary. 'Hell made her last effort, and all that is evil in creation, all the distortions of love and truth by which we are vexed, came surging down the estuary, and the boat hung motionless.' (223) Once again he hears the words 'The point of it...' as the boat speeds into the sunshine.

As a critique of liberalism 'The Point of It' is not without interest, but it is weakened by a lack of dramatic force and an incoherence of aim. Most of the dramatic interest comes at the beginning and end of the story, while the middle consists of a long, discursive account of Michael's career and is over-encumbered with characters. As for the story's aim, Forster's double desire to damn Michael and save him (a desire that probably reflects Forster's ambivalence toward Edwardian liberalism) may have been what provoked his Bloomsbury friends to ask, 'What *is* the point of it?' (Introduction, *Collected Tales*, viii) If, as the story asserts, 'there is nothing ultimate in Hell' and man 'will not lay aside all hope on entering it', Michael should be no more saveable than anyone else. Forster's uncertain perspective is reflected in his tone, which shifts from irony to sentimentality. Compare the following sneer at Michael's youthful belief in eternity with the lyrical treatment accorded his ultimate salvation:

Love, the love of humanity, warmed him; and even when he was thinking of other matters, was looking at Orion perhaps in the cold winter evenings,

a pang of joy, too sweet for description, would thrill him, and he would feel
sure that our highest impulses have some eternal value, and will be completed
hereafter. So full a nature could not brood over death. (203)

But what, after all, does the story show if not that Michael's
'highest impulses' did indeed have 'some eternal value'? And
why should he brood over death if, as the story suggests, the
hereafter may consist of a pleasant boat ride? The 'point of
it' may after all be that Forster wanted to throw out his cake
and eat it too.

The next two stories, 'Mr Andrews' and 'Co-ordination',
require little comment. 'Mr Andrews', which concerns the
ascent of two departed souls, a Christian and a Turk, to
Heaven and their experience there, is a pleasant blend of
comedy and pathos. Into a very short story, Forster manages
to contrast with amusing irony the morality of a Christian and
a Moslem and their expectations of the after-life, and to
introduce a spoof on the vicissitudes of religious faith.

'Co-ordination' expresses Forster's well-marked preference
for freedom and spontaneity to external control. Two old-maid
schoolteachers, Miss Haddon and her Principal, have been
'co-ordinating' the studies of their little girl pupils in order
to please the Board of Education but to the intense boredom
of the little girls themselves. Happening to pick up a seashell,
Miss Haddon hears in it the sounds of the sea; the Principal,
listening too, hears the sounds of a hunting party in a forest.
Both are sounds of an 'other kingdom', spelling freedom and
truth to the teachers and momentarily delivering them from
the bondage of time. Converted by their experience, they
declare an end to co-ordination and a school holiday during
which their charges play happy, disorganized games. For all
its humour, the story is more encumbered and less forceful
than 'Mr Andrews'. Not content to let it speak for itself,
Forster introduces a bit of a celestial whimsy, with 'Beethoven',
'Napoleon', and other heavenly figures commenting on the
'co-ordination' below. The mixture does not jell.

'The Story of a Siren' is of a different order from either
of the preceding pair. Combining Christian and classic myth,

it is a dark tale of spiritual suffering and the only one of Forster's in which a transcendent vision of truth and beauty is more of a curse than a blessing. Giuseppe, who after brutally beating his brother for refusing money from a party of tourists dives for money himself and sees the Siren, is haunted forever by a sense of the nullity of human life and action. In the depths of the sea, he finds a potentially fertilizing force, powerless to be reborn. Returning to land, he finds a spiritual desert. The effect of his experience on him is not unlike Mrs Moore's response to life after her visit to the Marabar Caves. Both suffer from spiritual exhaustion and sense the ultimate futility of human action.

> He would stand in the street looking at people, and the more he looked at them the more unhappy he became. When a child was born he would cover his face with his hands. If any one was married – he was terrible then, and would frighten them as they came out of church. (253)

His marriage to Maria, who has also according to rumour 'gone mad through bathing in the sea', fails to alleviate his misery. The villagers dislike them, partly at least because they seem bad for the tourist business. When Maria becomes pregnant, she and Giuseppe are to be sent inland, like Mary and Joseph before them; for the child, it is feared, will be the Antichrist, who will some day marry the Siren. But Maria is murdered instead, apparently by a priest. Giuseppe, alone and miserable, wanders about the world looking for someone else who has seen the Siren, and finally dies of tuberculosis in Liverpool. 'Never in my life', asserts his brother, 'will there be both a man and a woman from whom that child can be born, who will fetch up the Siren from the sea, and destroy silence, and save the world!' Eventually, however, the Siren will come up from the sea and sing, for 'silence and loneliness cannot last forever' (258).

To link the story's sensationalism and fantasy to the every-day world, Forster has provided a framework and a narrator. His narrator, an English tourist at Capri, hears it from Giuseppe's brother in the Blue Grotto, where they have been temporarily dropped by the narrator's boating party so that the young Italian might dive into the water and retrieve the narrator's dissertation on the Deist Controversy, which had accidentally fallen overboard. After retrieving the book, the brother proceeds to tell his story. When he has finished, the boating party returns. The narrator, who mediates between the world of the brother's story and the ordinary world, is carefully drawn. Susceptible to beauty and fantasy, he is nevertheless a rationalist who takes for granted the solid, familiar realities of his own world. Confronted with his companion's assertions about the Siren, he is naturally sceptical, a bit facetious, but curious. Whether the bent of his mind is suggested by his interest in deism may be open to question. In any event, his amusingly elaborate description of the dissertation sinking into the blue depths of the Mediterranean and assuming as it sinks all sorts of fantastic shapes, foreshadows his mind's submergence in the heady brew of the brother's story. That he hears the story in the Blue Grotto predisposes him to respond to it, for the Grotto appeals to him as 'a magic world, apart from all the commonplaces that are called reality', a 'world of blue' where 'only the fantastic would be tolerable' (248). The fantastic turns out to be more than tolerable, it is compelling: before the brother has finished his tale, the narrator has been led implicitly to question the nature of reality, and whether his own familiar world, so seemingly sure in its grasp of fact, is so very sure after all. 'The story of Giuseppe', he remarks, 'for all its absurdity and superstition, came nearer to reality than anything I had known before.' (254) Like Coleridge's wedding guest, he becomes, for the time being at least, both sadder and wiser. 'I don't know why, but it [the story] filled me with desire to help others – the greatest of all our desires, I suppose, and the most fruitless. The desire soon passed.' With the return of his companions, he will go back to the everyday world and presumably finish his book on the Deist Controversy, for he seems too shallow to be permanently changed by what he has heard. But the world to which he returns, as the story makes clear, is another 'heaven of the soft', a desert lacking secure spiritual foundations – an anticipation of Eliot's *Wasteland*. If the Siren will ever return to sing to it, it will probably be, to cite from *A Passage to India*, 'not yet...not there'.

While Forster's device of framing the story of Giuseppe and the Siren and supplying a narrator relates it to the everyday world, it also entails a liability. To hear the story from someone who hears it from someone who was himself little more than a passive witness to the crucial events almost inevitably entails a loss in immediacy of impact. As for Giuseppe, he emerges as a well-drawn Italian type, not as a rounded human being. Maria is totally undeveloped. Furthermore, because of the framing, our interest is necessarily shifted from the crucial events and the two characters most concerned with them to the narrator's response to the story. And since the narrator is a peripheral character who never sufficiently engages our sympathies, the story's impact is weakened.

No such liability attaches to the last story in the collection. 'The Eternal Moment', although a comparatively early tale, is one of Forster's most richly satisfying. Miss Raby, who in her middle age returns to the village near which she had once experienced an 'eternal moment', is a convincing combination of honesty, self-deceptiveness, naivety, warmth and detachment. She has mind and heart, she has the gift of friendship, and yet she is also, one feels, essentially solitary. Twenty years ago, when she was a girl, she had visited Vorta, near the Italian–Austrian border, and one day, while on a walk, had been amorously accosted by the young porter assigned to carry her things. Alarmed but not really displeased, she had repelled him, and only much later realized that the situation had constituted her 'eternal moment'. She had based a novel on it; the novel had put Vorta, then unspoiled, on the map – and spoiled it. Tourists came in, big hotels went up, commerce thrived. Now, accompanied by her friend Colonel Leyland and her maid, she returns to see how the place has changed.

Two changes are especially significant. The Albergo Biscione where she had stayed, and to which she returns, has been superseded in public favour by grander and more commercial establishments, in particular by the Grand Hôtel des Alpes, which is owned by the son of Signora Cantu, who owns the Biscione. The second and more significant change is in the handsome young porter who had tried to make love to her. He is now the stout, greasy, and middle-aged concierge of the Grand Hôtel des Alpes.

A well-intentioned, democratic woman, Miss Raby has thus managed, as she realizes, to cause grave social harm. To make partial restitution for the damage and assuage her conscience, she approaches Feo Ginori, the concierge, in order to recall him, if possible, to their eternal moment. The eternal moment for her was life: 'she had drawn unacknowledged power and inspiration from it, just as trees draw vigour from a subterranean spring' (300). Vorta, on the other hand, spells death. The hordes of tourists, the shopkeepers, the big hotels, have all but crushed the essential life of the place; and Feo, with his oily servility and professional smoothness, is the primary embodiment of the new Vorta, a kind of life-in-death. If, as Miss Raby feels, she can recall him to their supreme moment, she can save him. And she can also save herself, for she stands at the brink of old age and spiritual death. Her inspection of Vorta and her meeting with Signora Cantu, the refined owner of the now shabby Biscione, have made her feel that her life has been misspent, and that all that remains to her is to 'fold her hands and to wait, till her ugliness and her incompetence went the way of beauty and strength.' (289) But upon learning from the Signora that the concierge of the Grand Hôtel des Alpes is the very man who tried to make love to her on the mountainside, she suddenly revives, determined to see him that very afternoon.

Her sense of responsibility for Vorta and Feo is of course misguided. It is as absurd for her to blame herself for their 'destruction' as for the assassin of the Archduke Ferdinand to blame himself for the First World War and its aftermath. Feo, in any case, as the ensuing interview comically reveals, has not the slightest wish to be 'saved' by Miss Raby or anyone else. And Miss Raby is, to say the least, presumptious in trying to use Feo in order to mitigate her exaggerated sense of guilt.

The story comes to a head in a superb blend of comedy and pathos on the balcony of the Grand Hôtel, with Miss Raby trying to confront Feo with the facts of their common past. At first he remembers nothing, for this particular past is buried deep in his subconscious, just as the town's agrarian past is buried beneath its latter-day commercialism. When at last, through Miss Raby's persistent prompting, he does recall their meeting, it is with horror. What, he wonders, can be her motive in reminding him of it? Is she trying to ruin him professionally? Or is she – heaven forbid – in love with him? This last possibility flatters his vanity, but not enough to dispel his fear. She wants to save his soul, but he only wants to save his face. To Colonel Leyland, who appears in the course of the scene, it looks, as it does to Feo, as if a frustrated spinster is trying to stoke a dead furnace. To the hotel guests lucky enough to overhear, however imperfectly, the colloquy, it looks as if 'an Englishman had surprised his wife making love to the concierge'. As for Miss Raby, she is guilty of the very stupidity she deplores. If she cannot redeem Feo, perhaps at least, she suggests, he would let her adopt his youngest child.

He shall live among rich people. He shall see that they are not the vile creatures he supposes, always clamouring for respect and deference and trying to buy them with money. Rich people are good: they are capable of sympathy and love: they are fond of the truth; and when they are with each other they are clever. (303–4)

Such a combination of self-seeking and self-deception is worthy of Mrs Herriton or Herbert Pembroke, two of the prime goats in Forster's fiction; but that a woman as fundamentally frank and generous as Miss Raby should be guilty of it is the story's crowning irony.

Finally realizing the hopelessness of her effort, she desists. Feo is too much the official to be brought back to 'life', and Colonel Leyland too much the fool to see the truth. 'If Colonel Leyland also believed that she was now in love with Feo, she would not exert herself to undeceive him.' (306) Accordingly, she withdraws from the pair of them, leaving them, spiritually akin for all their difference in class, to contemplate her behaviour and the scandal that will certainly ensue.

But despite her failure to 'save' Feo, Miss Raby feels – and Forster apparently would have us believe – that she has at least 'lived worthily'. She has transformed her experience into art and thereby, in a sense, triumphed over it. She has also tried, whatever the results, to live honestly. She has 'given herself away' – intentionally risked making a fool of herself – in order to break down the barriers that divide class from class and restore a fellow human being to 'life'. It is a final irony that her very failure holds a qualified success: Leyland and Feo, divided though they are by class, feel a kinship.

Much as Colonel Leyland disliked touching people he took Feo by the arm, and then quickly raised his finger to his forehead.
'Exactly, sir,' whispered the concierge. 'Of course we understand – Oh, thank you, sir, thank you very much: thank you very much indeed!' (308)

The story's effectiveness does not depend on Miss Raby alone. Colonel Leyland and Feo, both of whom might have stepped from a nineteenth-century farce, are comparatively simple, but well drawn. The Colonel, stiff, class-conscious, morally unimaginative, and not unmindful of Miss Raby's wealth ('it lent an unacknowledged perfume to his thoughts') is humanized by his affection for her.

'Funny Lady!'
Close below him he could now see the white fragments of his sister's letter. In the valley the campanile appeared, rising out of wisps of silvery vapour.
'Dear Lady!' he whispered, making towards the village a little movement with his hands. (274)

Feo is the essence of the deferential petty official. With a sharp eye for the revealing gesture, Forster sets him before us,

He opened the windows, he filled the match-boxes, he flicked the little tables with a duster, always keeping an eye on the door in case any one arrived without luggage, or left without paying. He touched an electric bell, and a waiter flew up and cleared away Miss Raby's tea things. He touched another bell, and sent an underling to tidy up some fragments of paper which had fallen out of a bedroom window. Then 'Excuse me, madam!' and he had picked up Miss Raby's handkerchief with a slight bow. (292)

70

A flat character incapable of surprising us, Feo is comic in his rigidity, in his wholesale commitment to his role.

Another important factor in the story's success is Vorta itself. Once an agricultural village 'full of virility and power', it has become a miniature megalopolis destructive to human relationships. Its anomalous mixture of teutonic and latin culture, its hordes of tourists, its dedication to commerce and money, its vulgarity and pretentiousness, epitomize all that Forster dislikes about urban life. Only the new campanile in Vorta is beautiful. A symbolic reminder of the past and of transcendent aspiration, it nevertheless shares in the rootlessness of the town; for it has been built, as Feo points out, on a landslip, and will eventually fall.

What, finally, makes 'The Eternal Moment' superior to most of Forster's other stories is its moral and psychological complexity. Unlike some of the stories, it implies no pat moral judgements. It does not suggest that eternal moments are inevitably good, or that Miss Raby as a girl should have followed her instincts and run off with the porter, or that, returning to Vorta in her middle-age, she should have left well alone. Rather, it shows how intertwined in this world of ours good and evil can be. Miss Raby's moment, life-giving to her (because she did *not* follow her instinct), spells spiritual death to the town and the man she loved. And the town's present condition and the man's were promoted by 'ladies and gentlemen who were good and rich and often clever – who, if they thought about the matter at all, thought that they were conferring a benefit, moral as well as commercial, on any place in which they chose to stop' (284). Miss Raby's attempt to undo some of the damage she has inadvertently helped to create only embarrasses Feo and the Colonel and leads to her social and psychological isolation. If there is, then, a moral, it is, as Lionel Trilling pointed out in connection with Forster's fiction as a whole, that any attempt to live morally is full of pitfalls. But Forster's primary concern is not moral judgment but psychological exploration. To this end, he has eschewed the use of mythology – of pans, fauns, sirens, magic seashells and

71

haunted copses – for such devices inevitably emphasize wonder and mystery at the expense of the psychological. Instead he reveals the workings of Miss Raby's mind, and explores, ironically and dramatically, the clash between that mind and others. As a result, Miss Raby emerges as one of the most subtly drawn and convincing characters in Forster's fiction.

II

Of the fourteen stories in *The Life to Come*, four of them – all early – are in the spirit of several in the *Collected Tales*.[6] 'Ansell', the first, is a short, well-controlled tale of a young Cambridge scholar – the narrator – who, in losing the notes for his dissertation over a cliff ('The Story of a Siren'), is compelled to relinquish a promising academic career for the comparatively mindless pleasures of country life. Will he be better off? The narrator's ironic yet wistful response to the catastrophe leaves the answer in doubt, and may reflect Forster's mixed feelings toward the comparative values of gown and country.

A longer and more elaborate tale is 'Albergo Empedocle', Forster's first published work of fiction. Like 'The Story of a Panic' and 'The Road from Colonus', it deals with the spirit of place; and the place in question is Sicily – the Sicily of dilapidated Greek temples where Empedocles proclaimed his belief in the transmigration of souls.

Forster's travellers are Sir Edwin and Lady Peaslake, their two daughters Lilian and Mildred, and Mildred's fiancé, Harold. The parents are stodgy; Lilian shows glimmerings of imagination but is unformed; Mildred is energetic and intellectual. Armed with a Baedeker, she travels through Europe collecting facts. But she is no 'dry encyclopaedia. Her appetite for facts was balanced by her reverence for imagination.' Harold, on the other hand, shows none of her zeal for facts.

---

[6] The fourteenth story, 'Three Courses and a Dessert', which originally appeared in *Wine and Food*, is not considered here. Forster contributed only one of the 'courses', the second; the other two being by Christopher Dilke and A. E. Coppard. James Laver wrote 'The Dessert'.

He simply follows the Peaslakes on their rounds, and, suffering from insomnia, is too tired much of the time to care where he is or what he sees. To Mildred's regret, he seems almost entirely unimaginative. Almost entirely; for he has one trick that shows promise: to put himself to sleep he pretends to be someone else. 'I just say to myself, "That's someone lying awake. Why doesn't he go to sleep if he's tired?" Then he – I mean I – do, and it's all right.' (13)[7]

Harold's trick precipitates the crisis. Having fallen asleep one morning among the sunbaked ruins of Acragas, he wakes up convinced that he had once, in a former life, lived there. Mildred is thrilled. At long last Harold is showing imagination. More than that, as she devoutly brings herself to believe, he has indeed been there before: in his past life he was an ancient Greek. Inspired by his state, she tries to project herself into the past. Surely she too had been a Greek. Surely she too had once lived in Acragas. But her belief is cruelly dispelled when Harold whispers into her ear, 'No Mildred, darling, you have not.' (26)

Shattered in spirit, Mildred calls him a charlatan; and now it is his turn to be shattered, for Mildred no longer believes in him. He sobs, faints, recovers, falls, faints again and comes to, muttering in a curious thick voice about wine, conjurers, a flute girl, porters, and other elements from his past life. Never regaining his 'sanity', he is incarcerated in an asylum. Like other Forsterian visionaries, he cannot connect his imaginative world with that of mundane reality. Classical scholars test him and prove to their satisfaction that he is mad. Only his friend Tommy – the story's narrator – believes in him. 'I firmly believe that he has been a Greek – nay, that he is a Greek, drawn by recollection back into his previous life . . . And I also believe, that if things had happened otherwise, he might be living that greater life among us, instead of among friends of two thousand years ago, whose names we have never heard. That is why I shall never forgive Mildred Peaslake as long as I live.' (35)

[7] All page references in *The Life to Come and Other Stories* are from the Arnold, 1972 edition.

Is Harold mad or sane? Has he, as Mildred's parents think, simply suffered a bad case of sunstroke, or has he, as Mildred at first believes, had a genuine vision of his past life? Should one accept the sunstroke explanation and thereby ally oneself with Mildred's stuffy parents, or should one go along with Harold, who is clearly unbalanced and an intellectual dullard to boot? It is typical of Forster's irony that the story should raise such questions without suggesting that the reader should weigh them seriously. As in some of the other tales, the supernatural is introduced as a teasing possibility, an idea to be entertained but not unequivocally accepted. Forster's attitude here is in tune with that of other Edwardian writers – with Beerbohm's, for example, and 'Saki's' – whose taste for fantasy may be viewed as an antidote to too many heavy doses of late-Victorian realism, but who are themselves too much a product of a science-minded, materialistic culture to give complete credence to spiritualistic explanations of the unseen. Even in so spiritually directed a novel as *A Passage to India*, Forster is careful to provide a possible physical explanation for Mrs Moore's vision in the Marabar Caves. Before she went into the cave, she felt tired and poorly and might, he suggests, have sat in the sun too long. Just so with Harold: he too was tired and went to sleep in the sun. Hence one can interpret his vision, like Mrs Moore's, to suit the bent of one's mind.

If the supernatural is introduced as a teasing possibility in 'Albergo Empedocle', its presence is unequivocal in 'The Purple Envelope'. A mixture of hocus-pocus and social satire, it contains more mystification and incident than necessary to show how Howard Sholton, an unrefined youth who likes to hunt and kill ('as all those do who are really in touch with nature'), finally inherits the family estate – a home to which he is spiritually more attuned than is the cultivated and pompous uncle who has fraudulently laid claim to it. The story contains some amusing satire of aging country house types, but lacks the kind of wholesale commitment to the supernatural that a good ghost story requires.

'The Helping Hand' is an amusing but atypical story about

an art historian whose lifelong work on an eminent Renaissance artist, Giovanni da Empoli, is anticipated – and dis-
torted – in a small, popular book on the subject by a lady to
whom Mr Henderson, the historian, had casually lent his
notes. Among Forster's stories 'The Helping Hand' is unique
as the only one not concerned with an opposition of different
levels of experience or different orders of value.

More representative and provocative is 'The Rock'. One of
the few stories of Forster's to have been directly inspired by
his visit to a particular place, its narrator reports his conversation with a woman about the most crucial incident in her life
and her husband's which occurred when the latter, sailing his
boat off the coast of Cornwall, is washed onto a rock and, just
as he is about to slip back into the sea, is rescued by fishermen.
Because of his narrow escape, the couple feel their love renewed, their lives transfigured – 'everything transfigured because he had been saved'. How, then, should the husband
reward his rescuers? This is the question that haunts him. Give
them money? They are poor and could certainly use it. But
the husband cannot accept such a crass, though practical,
solution; for the value of life, and especially of one
transfigured, cannot be measured in money. And so he decides
to give them nothing – nothing, that is, but himself. Selling all
his assets, he casts himself penniless on the charity of his
rescuers, who at first regard him as mad but eventually come
to accept him.

Although not quite the 'complete flop' that Forster describes it as being, 'The Rock' is not dramatic and forceful
enough for its theme – a theme that preoccupies Forster
throughout his fiction – the problem of spiritual salvation. In
selling his assets and casting himself on the charity of his
rescuers, the husband is in effect, trying to save his soul.

Has he succeeded? It is a question on which the narrator
appears divided. On the one hand he espouses the practical
view that the fishermen should have been rewarded with
money; on the other, he accedes to the wife's view that the
worth of a human life cannot be measured in money. 'I told

myself that this was fluid, unsubstantial stuff. But in my heart I knew that she and all that she said was a rock in the tideway.' Finally, the narrator declares that the husband's brand of salvation is not for him. 'Such adventures may profit the disembodied soul, but as long as I have flesh and blood I pray that my grossness preserve me. Our lower nature has its dreams. Mine is of a certain farm, windy but fruitful, halfway between the deserted moorland and the uninhabitable sea.'

The narrator's mixed feelings reflect, I think, Forster's. A humanist but not a Christian, Forster cannot fully accept the traditional Christian prescription for saving one's soul – to give up the world and turn to Christ. Salvation lies rather, Forster often suggests, in a loving acceptance of the world and in the fulfilment of one's sexual and emotional needs. By accepting Gino as his friend, Philip Herriton, in effect, accepts life and is 'saved'. Similarly, by marrying the socially un-acceptable George Emerson, Lucy Honeychurch achieves her salvation.

Yet the world, as Forster often indicates, is a dangerous sea, full of rocks and reefs ready to shipwreck the unwary. Even personal relationships are uncertain, depending as they do upon trust and reliability. Hence, I think, Forster's demon-strable attraction to a mode of salvation that looks not to this world but to the transcendent – to an order that transcends worldly flux and to art as an expression of order. Looking beyond people and personal relationships, Philip Herriton worships art and an idealized vision of Italy. Rickie Elliot harbours a Shelleyan ideal of the brotherhood of man and venerates his dead mother as a symbol of truth and beauty. A love of absolute truth and justice leads Helen Schlegel to crusade for Leonard Bast. Mrs Moore is inspired by a semi-mystical feeling for the divine; and Professor Godbole seems most at home when contemplating eternity. Most of Forster's fiction, including 'The Rock', reflects his ambivalence toward the two modes of salvation: that which looks to the world, and that which looks beyond it.

The remaining stories in ' *The Life to Come* ' deal with homosexuality. Of these, five are fairly serious; and three, comic and jocular. In all eight of the stories the main characters become caught between the 'straight' world on the one hand and the homosexual on the other – two forces, two levels of experience, whose contrary demands the characters should, ideally, be able to reconcile. Forster's protagonists are invariably associated with the straight world. As respected members of established society, they are never completely committed to homosexuality. One gets married in the course of the story; one is on his wedding trip; one keeps a mistress; one is said to be 'addicted to women.'[8] Their homosexual partners, on the other hand, come from outside the established class and therefore (by a logic generally applicable to Forster's fictive world) possess an alien vigour and spontaneity. Like the mythological figures in Forster's early stories and such characters in the novels as George Emerson and Gino Carella, they expose the protagonist to a more vital level of experience than the one to which he is accustomed.

The title story, 'The Life to Come', is one of the best. Like *A Passage to India* it shows how an institutional force can corrupt the individual and weaken the purely human ties between men. In 'The Life to Come' the institutional force is Christianity. The human tie is the homosexual passion between the Reverend Paul Pinmay, a missionary, and Vithobai, a young African chief whom he converts to Christianity. Both characters are brilliantly drawn. Pinmay is a bureaucratic and pious humbug who fitfully tries to express his submerged humanity – a young Herbert Pembroke in clerical garb. Vithobai, one of the most vivid of Forster's natives, is a convincing mixture of pride, craft and naivety.

Irony is pervasive. Probably the most piquant example of it is Vithobai's repeated taking of Pinmay's injunction to him to 'come to Christ' as an invitation to buggery. But its primary target is the way in which institutional Christianity, working

---

[8] Pinmay gets married in 'The Life to Come'; Ernest, in 'The Obelisk', is on his wedding trip; Dr Bonifaz Schpiltz is married and has a mistress in 'What Does it Matter? A Morality'; Sir Richard Conway in 'Arthur Snatchfold' is 'addicted to women'.

hand in hand with European imperialism, contributes to the spiritual and economic impoverishment of its converts. Not only does Christian imperialism undermine the bond between Pinmay and Vithobai, it saps the area of its native vitality. Dancing is put down; trees are felled to make way for mines; the mines employ natives to work underground; previously unknown diseases are introduced for which new hospitals are erected. 'Can't you grasp, Barnabas [Vithobai],' remarks Pinmay, 'that under God's permission certain evils attend civilization, but that if men do God's will the remedies for the evils keep pace?' (74) Significantly, Pinmay marries the sister of a rich local mine owner. Vithobai, on the other hand, is content to marry beneath him 'a native catechist from the adjoining valley' whom the missionaries had selected for him. Ironically all these signs of spiritual decline follow from the one 'good' act that the story records, the passionate love between the two men. One is reminded of the commercialism that comes to Vorta as a result of Miss Raby's 'eternal moment'.

Good as it is, 'The Life to Come' is marred by a few implausibilities. The ending, for example, in which the dying Vithobai stabs Pinmay through the heart, then leaps to his own death from the roof of his house, is psychologically unlikely and aesthetically out-of-key. It is odd, too, that, after the two men make love, Pinmay seems unconcerned that Vithobai might betray the affair to the white community. Finally, one may remark the unlikely fact that Vithobai's marriage and increasing responsibilities to his family over a ten-year period seem to have no effect on his feeling for Pinmay. Here and there Forster strains the material to serve his subject.

No such straining is evident in 'Dr Woolacott'. Probably of more limited appeal to the modern reader, it is a strange melange of fantasy and reality reflected through the consciousness of Clesant, a young country squire afflicted with an illness unspecified but obviously psychosomatic. Under the care of Dr Woolacott, he must give up the violin and avoid excitement or anything that might tire him. Above all he must not be 'intimate with people'. If he follows this regimen, he may, he feels, live on for years. In short, he may continue to live a life-in-death, buried in the shell of his sickly but sensitive mind.

Into Clesant's consciousness as he sits in his garden listening to distant voices and watching the 'colourless shapeless country people', a young farm-worker comes. Is he real, or a figment of Clesant's imagination? As with everything that Clesant perceives, we cannot be sure. The farm-worker is sympathetic when Clesant tells him of his illness, but when he mentions the name of Dr Woolacott, the farm-worker, admitting to knowing the doctor, abruptly turns on his heels and leaves.

The scene shifts to the gun-room in Clesant's house – a room that, like its owner, is a mere sickly reminder of a vital past: instead of guns, trophies and fishing rods, its shelves and cupboards now contain medicine bottles and air cushions. Full of 'languorous yearning', Clesant is alone on the sofa waiting for tea. Suddenly the farm-worker enters, dressed this time 'in good if somewhat provincial clothes, with a pleasant and resolute expression upon his face'. They talk, have tea, and then, inevitably, make love. But the love-making is brought to a sudden, premature halt when the farm-worker, kissing Clesant, murmurs, 'And to hell with Woolacott.' Just as he was forgetting himself, Clesant is jolted back to the knowledge that he is sick. What, he wonders, has the young farm-worker got against Woolacott? During the ensuing conversation the farm-worker reveals that he knew the doctor in France during the war, that no one the doctor treated ever got well, and that he, the farm-worker, was badly wounded and recovered only because he refused to let Woolacott treat him. Clesant, he insists, must 'sack Woolacott'. When Clesant indicates that he cannot do this, his friend, disappointed, starts to leave, but, hearing voices in the hall, returns in a state of alarm. He cannot meet the others in the house – 'they've heard of something I did out in France' – and asks to be hidden. Helping him into a cupboard, Clesant determines to betray him when the others come in by pretending to have trapped him there on purpose.

The voices enter, speaking of the sounds of a mysterious violin playing somewhere in the house – but where?

Playing all sorts of music, gay, grave, passionate. But never completing a theme. Always breaking off. A beautiful instrument. Yet so unsatisfying... leaving the hearers much sadder than if it had never been performed. What was the use (someone asked) of music like that? Better silence absolute than this aimless disturbance of our peace. (93)

Feeling the familiar illness returning, Clesant writhes in convulsions, but retains his new feeling of love long enough to cry, 'Don't go to the cupboard, no one's there.' And no one, as it turns out, is there. 'It was as it had always been since his father's death – shallow, tidy, a few medicine bottles on the upper shelf, a few cushions stored on the lower.' (93)

In the final scene Clesant, delirious, engages in a dialogue with his disease, which accuses him of 'intimacy' and declares the farm-worker an illusion whom Clesant created because he wanted to feel attractive. Prepared to give up the farm-worker in exchange for a long but sickly life, Clesant nevertheless resists the notion that he is only an illusion. He struggles with his disease, which begins 'to crouch and gurgle' and then fall. The nightmare passes and he hears again the voice of his friend begging him to come with him – 'for an evening to my earthly lodging'. As the voice grows stronger, Clesant struggles, 'but whether to reach or elude the hovering presence he did not know. There was always a barrier either way, always his own nature.' Suddenly the lights of a car. It is Dr Woolacott at last. Clesant hides the now frightened ghost of his love in his bed; and as the doctor, 'leading his army', enters, Clesant and his 'illusion' entwine and kiss. And then 'something gashed him where life had concentrated, and Dr Woolacott, arriving too late, found him dead on the floor'. Examining the room, the doctor recalls a hospital ward in France and his voice saying to a recruit, 'Do let me patch you up, oh but you must just let me patch you up...'

Unique among Forster's stories in its suggestive use of symbolism, allegory, and fantasy, 'Dr Woolacott' invites and resists interpretation. On one level it presents a vision of a meaningless, postwar, upper-class country life, artificially sustained and capable perhaps of surviving in sickly fashion for many years. More broadly interpreted it deals with postwar England, or Europe, or the world – a place to which not even art, as symbolized by the violin, can speak. Clesant's estate is a countrified version of Eliot's Wasteland, and the voices discussing the fragmentary sounds of the violin remind one of the women in Prufrock's life who 'come and go / Talking of Michelangelo'. Clesant is an egocentric and lonely youth trapped between life and death, or, perhaps more accurately, by a life-and-death wish, and struggling for a salvation that can only be gained through love. The love is narcissistic and homosexual, and the lover fears that it may be revealed to an uncomprehending world.

Unlike 'Dr Woolacott', 'Arthur Snatchfold', the story that follows, is quite explicit. Sir Richard Conway, a bored businessman on a country weekend, buggers a milkman in the shrubbery, only to learn several weeks later, while lunching in London with his former host, that because of the escapade the milkman has been arrested and sentenced to prison. If he had only divulged his partner's identity, he might have received a lighter punishment; but this he refused to do. So there it is. Sir Richard, who has two daughters and a respectable reputation, is safe. Taking a notebook from his pocket, he writes down the name of his lover – 'yes, his lover who was going to prison to save him, in order that he might forget it. Arthur Snatchfold. He had only heard the name once, and he would never hear it again.'

The next three stories are light and amusing. The first, 'The Obelisk', concerns a couple of honeymooners at a seaside resort – Ernest, a schoolteacher, who is small and precise; and Hilda, a typist, who is big and romantic. On their way to the Obelisk, a local attraction, they pair up with a couple of sailors and find, through mutual deception, a fulfilment that up to then has eluded them. Hilda feels revived. She can face her home and husband with a new freshness; and Ernest is infused with a guarded gaiety.

'What Does it Matter? A Morality' is another spoof, and a delightful one that makes some telling points about the difference between true morality and sham, and the relation between public life and private. Sex is the issue. And, as soon as the Pottibakians acknowledge that sex is natural and fun – even when it is 'unnatural' – they become spiritually liberated and morally enlightened. The Republic of Pottibakia, in other words, achieves that connection between the outer life and the inner that the Schlegels desire in *Howards End*.

In 'The Classical Annex' a Romanstatue of a gladiator in a provincial museum comes to life and violates the curator's son. The story contains some pointed ridicule of how unenlightened people look at art, but it is otherwise little more than a protracted joke.

The last two stories are more serious and ambitious. The first, 'The Torque', which is set in the early Christian period, is strong enough to make one wonder why it is Forster's only piece of historical fiction. As in 'The Life to Come', the opposition with which it deals is between sex and Christianity. Marcian, a boy of about seventeen with healthy animal instincts, belongs to an established landowner's family, all of them Christians. His sister Perpetua, a fastidious and determined girl, has taken a vow of perpetual virginity, and the story opens with the scene of her dedication ceremony – brilliantly described – in the small family basilica. Conspicuous among the church's decorations is a barbaric torque of gold, a reminder, according to the presiding bishop, of a recent miracle. Five days ago, returning from a visit to a holy matron, Perpetua and her party were attacked by Goths, and just as Perpetua was about to be raped, God heard her prayer. Thunder and lightning flashed, her would-be ravisher staggered back, and, overcome with repentance, offered the torque in atonement.

Hearing this story Marcian emits an involuntary and embarrassing laugh, for he alone knows the truth; and it is what he knows that provides, by means of a flashback, much of the substance of Forster's story. In summary, Marcian rather than God was responsible for the 'miracle'. Defending his sister from the Goths' attack, it was he who was raped by their leader, Euric, who later draped the torque round his neck in appreciation.

Now Marcian is in love with Euric. The night after the dedication ceremony he has an erotic dream – described in some of the worst prose in Forster's fiction – of mounting Euric in the basilica and riding him naked around the interior: 'Heaven opened and he rode like a devil, his head down, his heels in the air . . . They flew round and round the basilica and defiled it, they shot through its roof into the storm-torn night. There was a blinding lightning flash . . .' (163) He wakes to a real storm outside and sees the basilica flickering as if on fire. Perpetua, robed in white, appears. Determined to save 'her people' and scorning her brother's entreaties to take care, she enters the building. A thunderbolt falls, and Church and girl are reduced to ashes. The event signals the end of ecclesiastical rule in the area. Life becomes productive and happy; and Marcian, who never sees Euric again, is content to remain at home, a pleasure to his aging parents. He sleeps with his horse, aptly named Euric, and charges on it around the countryside.

'The Torque' vividly conveys the spirit and atmosphere of its period. The characters are human and yet historical. Marcian is certainly more believable than some of Forster's other 'natural' young men, and Perpetua is well drawn. Yet, despite is virtues, 'The Torque' does not measure up to Forster's best fiction; mainly, I think, because the author fails to involve the characters in complicated relationships and issues. The most crucial event, Marcian's contact with Euric, fizzles out in a wet dream; and Christianity is exploded before it can be a real force. Under the circumstances, it is hardly surprising that the ending is, as Oliver Stallybrass remarks, 'perfunctory'.

'The Other Boat', the last story entirely by Forster in the collection, is the best. Probably finished as late as 1958, it displays a power and finesse worthy of the author of *A Passage to India*. Its protagonist, Lionel March, a young army captain on his way by boat to India to marry his fiancée and take up a post, has a homosexual affair with his cabin-mate, a half-caste

"The Other Boat"

boy named Cocoanut – an affair that ends tragically when Lionel, fearful of the effect on his career of almost certain discovery, strangles Cocoanut, then commits suicide by diving into the Red Sea.

The story's force derives from every one of its elements – the careful characterization of the two principals and the supporting characters, the story's style, structure, and choice of incidents, and its ironic foreshadowings and deployment of 'echoes'.

The attraction between Lionel and Cocoanut is largely an attraction of opposites. Superficially viewed Lionel, with his 'thick fairish hair, blue eyes, glowing cheeks...strong white teeth...and broad shoulders', is a recruiting poster's dream. His voice is quiet, 'his demeanour assured, his temper equable'. Having acquitted himself with dash and decision by killing a man in a desert war, he has won his captaincy early and the respect of his fellow officers. His virile appearance and manner attract women, and Cocoanut.

Beneath Lionel's superficial sang-froid, however, all is not quite so cool. The dash and decision that he displayed in war is, from another point of view, impetuous brutality, and as such underlies the murder of Cocoanut. Like certain other Forsterian heroes, moreover, Lionel is shadowed, if not exactly dominated, by his mother, a puritannically high-minded woman whose distaste for sex drove her husband – Lionel's father – into running off with a native girl when he was in the army in India, and partly accounts for Lionel's major psychological weakness, his sexual insecurity. Cocoanut's successful seduction of Lionel is largely due to Cocoanut's being, surprisingly, the very first person to make him feel physically attractive. 'Hitherto he had been ashamed of being built like a brute: his preceptors had condemned carnality or had dismissed it as a waste of time, and his mother had ignored its existence in him and all her children; being hers, they had to be pure.' (180) Lionel's insecurity makes him especially susceptible to the various reinforcements with which Cocoanut artfully follows up the seduction: the gifts, the payment of

gambling debts, and the hush-money to stewards and
Cocoanut's servant. Only dimly does Lionel grow to sense
that, under Cocoanut's spell, he becomes, in effect, a male
prostitute.

Cocoanut is superbly drawn. Of mixed but indeterminate
ancestry, he is devious, intuitive, and perceptive, living by his
wits in a world committed to tips and bribes. He skips about
like a monkey, and speaks a lingo peculiarly his own:

'Man, shall we now perhaps have our cigarette?' (178)
'But she – she saw me only, running in the sun with my devil's head, and m'm
m'm m'm all you follow me till the last one the tiny one dies, and she, she
talking to an officer, a handsome one, oh to sleep in his arms as I shall in
yours, so she forgets the sun and it strikes the tiny one. I see.' (185)

His passion for Lionel is genuine and deep. He wants to pry
him away from his career and his fiancée, to know and
control him, to possess him exclusively.

All his life he had wanted a toy that would not break, and now he was
planning how he would play with Lionel for ever. He had longed for him
ever since their first meeting, embraced him in dreams when only that was
possible, met him again as the omens foretold, and marked him down, spent
money to catch him and lime him, and here he lay, caught, and did not know
it. (174)

The world from which Cocoanut wants to take Lionel is that
of the British colonializer. Forster's depiction of the type is as
vivid and devastating as it was in *A Passage to India*. In the
following passage, for example, in which Lionel tries to anticipate discovery by telling his British companions on the S.S.
Normannia about his cabinmate, sharp satire fuses with tragic
foreshadowing:

'I got a passage all right,' he brayed, 'but at the cost of sharing my cabin with
a wog.' All condoled, and Colonel Arbuthnot in the merriest of moods
exclaimed, 'let's hope the blacks don't come off on the sheets,' and Mrs
Arbuthnot, wittier still, cried, 'Of course they won't, dear, if it's wog it'll be
the coffees.' Everyone shouted with laughter, the good lady basked in the
applause, and Lionel could not understand why he suddenly wanted to throw
himself into the sea. (175)

Lionel rebels against the world of supercilious British coloniaー
lizers, to which he belongs, and without which, as he comes

85

to realize too late, he has nothing. 'The Other Boat' is essen-tially about a man who becomes alienated from one order of experience by another, and is finally unable to give himself to either.

The story is superbly developed. The opening scene, a prologue, is set aboard the boat (the *other* boat) on which Lionel had travelled as a boy with his brothers, sisters and mother from India to England after the scandal of his father's dere-liction – the boat on which he had met Cocoanut, and the children had all played together. The scene is crucial, showing as it does how the passion between the two young men had its roots in childhood and providing grounds for Mrs March's dislike of Cocoanut, a source of subsequent anxiety for Lionel. Elements from the opening scene are ironically referred to in later parts of the story, of which one example will suffice. Cocoanut leads the children in an incomprehensible game that one of them wrongly identifies as 'Noah's Ark'. The game comes to nothing, and only toward the end of the story, when Cocoanut asks Lionel to kiss him, is it recalled:

'Kiss me.'

'No.'

'Noah? No? Then I kiss you.' (195)

It is a minor echo, but one that, nevertheless, indicates that the roots of coming disaster lie in the distant past.

From the prologue the story leaps forward to Lionel's letter to his mother ('Hullo the Mater'), written aboard the *Nor-mannia*, in which he tries to throw dust in her eyes by telling her how Cocoanut, 'influential in shipping circles', managed to get him a cabin, 'single berth', on a completely booked ship. 'He is on board too, but our paths seldom cross. He has more than a touch of the tar brush, so consorts with his own dusky fraternity, no doubt to their mutual satisfaction.' (171) After posting the letter he plays bridge with his English companions, 'the Big Eight', then goes to his cabin, where Cocoanut is waiting. The affair is in full swing. For the purpose of irony Forster has plunged us *in medias res* before going back to the beginning of the voyage and showing, with psychological

86

insight, how Cocoanut gradually undermines Lionel's initially
outraged resistance and brings him to bed. Having accomplished this, he makes Lionel his enraptured slave. Only one
thing threatens to disturb the relationship – Lionel's fear of
discovery.

Matters come to a head one night in the cabin when they
are about to make love and Lionel notices that the door is
unlocked. Accusations and protestations ensue, followed by an
uneasy truce, but the magic of the moment is dispelled. To
regain his balance and try to plan his future, Lionel goes on
deck, where most of his fellow passengers, because of the heat,
are sleeping. Colonel Arbuthnot, one of the Big Eight, awakes,
and in the course of the conversation offhandedly remarks that
'the resident wog' is in trouble for having allegedly bribed his
way on board and into Lionel's cabin. '...if the Company
thinks it can treat a British officer like that it's very much
mistaken. I'm going to raise hell at Bombay.' Suddenly Lionel
knows himself adrift – alienated from the English and unable
to keep with Cocoanut. With a disgusted exclamation he
returns to his cabin, determined at least to get a good night's
sleep in his own upper berth. But during his absence on deck
Cocoanut has moved into it. All right, he would go back on
deck and sleep there till the voyage was over. 'He must keep
with his own people, or he would perish.' When Cocoanut
leans over and bites Lionel's arm, drawing blood, in retaliation
for the latter's refusal to kiss him, the catastrophe is at hand:

> The sweet act of vengeance followed, sweeter than ever for both of them,
> and as ecstasy hardened into agony his hands twisted the throat. Neither of
> them knew when the end came, and when he realized it felt no sadness, no
> remorse. It was part of a curve that had long been declining, and had nothing
> to do with death. He covered again with his warmth and kissed the closed
> eyelids tenderly and spread the bright-coloured scarf. Then he burst out of
> the stupid cabin onto the deck, and naked and with the seeds of love on him
> he dived into the sea. (195–6)

The English try to hush up the scandal, but Lionel's mother
receives his letter and 'never mentioned his name again'.

Lionel March's passage to India, like the journeys of other

Forsterian travellers, exposes him to two levels of experience, one familiar, the other new. The familiar level corresponds with what Forster in *Howards End* calls the outer life; the new level, with the inner life; and, as in *Howards End* the question is, can the two levels be reconciled? Lionel's suicide, of course, stems from his realization that they cannot be. It is either his own kind or Cocoanut, but not both – and he desperately needs both.

III

'The Other Boat', together with Forster's other homosexual fiction, testifies to his interest in the problem the homosexual faces in trying to adjust his needs to the demands of society. Forster's interest in this problem, moreover, must have sharpened, if it does not completely underlie, the preoccupation he shows throughout his fiction with the impact of new levels of experience upon his characters.

Most of the stories in the *Collected Tales* and *The Life to Come* illustrate this preoccupation. And many of them involve their characters in a journey that takes them from their usual world to one that extends their idea of reality. Miss Raby's girlhood trip to the Alps, Harold's to Sicily and a former life, Mr Lucas's visit to Greece, and Lionel March's voyage to the Red Sea – these and other journeys introduce the travellers to new orders of experience that they must try to assimilate and connect with the everyday world. That so many of them, however, fail to make the connection reflects Forster's appraisal of the modern world as one in which the demands of the outer and inner life can seldom be harmonized.

4

A Room With a View

Forster's third novel, *A Room with a View*, is less ambitious and better controlled than *The Longest Journey*, and most readers like it more. Unlike *The Longest Journey*, it is an overtly romantic novel, a love story whose heroine, after trying from a sense of propriety to ignore her love for a socially questionable young man, finally marries him, and, so far as we can determine, lives happily ever after. More than Forster's other four novels, it recalls Jane Austen. With due allowance for changes of fashion and idiom, most of the characters might have stepped from the pages of one of her books, and Summer Street, the home of the heroine and her family, is the sort of quiet English village about which she wrote – Highgate or Longbourn – a century later. Forster's novel, too, displays a gift for satire and comedy that recalls the art of the earlier novelist.

Yet *A Room with a View* is wider in scope than any of Jane Austen's novels. Its heroine Lucy Honeychurch travels to Italy where she encounters a spirit totally new to her. Wilder and freer than the spirit of Summer Street and her home Windy Corner, it embraces beauty, passion, violence, and love; and it makes an indelible impression on Lucy. Not only does she acquire a new view of the world, she becomes involved in a new life. The result is that try as she does to return to the old view and the old life, she cannot. They no longer fulfil her needs, and she cannot be happy until she accepts the new.

In another respect, too, the novel goes beyond one of Jane Austen's, for it reaches out beyond Lucy and her social environment toward the unseen and the infinite. It pits the genteel pretensions of village life against the mystery of life itself. Envisioning man in a disjointed, inexplicable universe, it implicitly searches for some means of gaining a sense of wholeness and harmony, a sense that the inner life and the outer can be attuned.

As for Lucy, she is warm, artless, and likeable. She has none of Philip Herriton's supercilious worldliness, none of Rickie Elliot's introverted and visionary sensibility. Yet she has something in common with both these characters. Like them, she is unsure of herself and more inclined to be swayed by the conventional attitudes of her class than by her own instincts and desires. The sheltered product of a well-to-do family, she has been surrounded by rich, pleasant people who, so far as she is concerned, constitute life. Like Peter Pan, she is resistant to change. She wants to remain a child, to dwell forever in the security of her family at Windy Corner, Summer Street. Yet change, as the novel suggests, is inevitable. The vicissitudes of the weather and the passage of the seasons ironically counterpoint Lucy's attempts to stay as she is. Going to Florence in the spring, she experiences fair weather and foul. She falls in love with a young man, but, warring against the spring within her, tries not to recognize the fact. Instead she returns to Summer Street and tries to hold on to her old life, to a kind of eternal summer. But with the advent of autumn and stormy weather, her crisis comes to a head. Meeting it, she triumphs and returns to Italy – this time happily married – the following spring. Her triumph is partly due to her own nature, partly to good luck. Despite her resistance to change, she has a streak of the rebel and a sense of adventure, two qualities that predispose her to break through the shell of convention in which she is encased. But she is also, like Rickie Elliot, a victim of circumstances: she is caught in a network of forces over which she has little or no control. Luckily things turn out well for her, but they might have, as for Rickie or for her chaperon-cousin Charlotte Bartlett, have turned out badly.

All seems safe enough when she and Charlotte arrive at the Pension Bertolini in Florence. The pension, despite its name, is militantly English. The clientele are English, the landlady speaks with a cockney accent, and portraits of 'the late Queen and the late Poet Laureate' hang in the dining room, along with a notice of the English church under the direction of the Reverend Cuthbert Eager, M.A. Oxon. But there is a disquieting note. Lucy and Charlotte, tired from the trip, voice their disappointment to one another in the dining room that, contrary to the landlady's promise, they have not been given rooms with a view – a view, that is, of the Arno. Their complaint is overheard by the other guests, one of whom, an elderly man, addresses them with the information that he and his son have views and would be glad, he implies, to exchange rooms with them. Charlotte is startled. A prim, middle-aged spinster, she has long since rejected 'life' for convention, and serves as a warning to Lucy not to do likewise. What right has this man to address them? 'Generally at a pension people looked them over for a day or two before speaking, and often did not find out that they would "do" till they had gone.' (4–5)[1] Obviously the old man is ill-bred. He is, as she and Lucy are soon to learn, Mr Emerson, a Forsterian sage and a spokesman for passion and honesty, whose chief role in the novel will be to warn Lucy against 'muddle' and help save her from disaster. His son George, who is in the dining room with him, espouses his father's philosophy, though with one difference. Where the father looks on the positive side of life and preaches the gospel of *carpe diem*, the son is haunted by a sense that the world is out of joint and life without ultimate meaning. Tacked to the wall of his room is a large question mark representing the Everlasting Why. 'Make my boy think like us,' the father will plead to Lucy the very next day. 'Make him realize that by the side of the everlasting Why there is a Yes – a transitory Yes if you like, but a Yes.' (32) Clearly, then, George will need Lucy for his salvation as she will need him. More than any of the other characters, the two Emersons oppose the conventionalism that threatens Lucy. Reality for them lies not so much in society as in nature and in the mysterious universe beyond our vision, in what Forster often calls the unseen. Together they help give the novel a metaphysical dimension.

---

[1] All page references in *A Room With a View* are from the Vintage Books (Knopf and Random House), New York, edition.

Despite Charlotte's reluctance to talk to strange men, she and Lucy are persuaded to change rooms with the Emersons, and thus Lucy acquires her room with a view. She will soon learn, however, that life means more than rooms and views: it means participation. The Florence that she looks out on from the security of her bedroom window is more than a city of art and monuments for which a Baedeker can serve as sufficient guide, it is a city of life – and death. The very next morning when she finds herself adrift in Santa Croce without her Baedeker, it is a symbolic warning that she will need more than a book to guide her.

Besides the Emersons, Lucy meets other individuals at the pension who will help to determine the course of her life. There is the Reverend Arthur Beebe, a detached and perceptive bachelor, who sees in Lucy a potentiality for development and in Charlotte a hint of 'strangeness' that might belie her prim old-maidishness. He is right on both counts. Lucy will develop, and Charlotte will display a latent sympathy with her and George instrumental in eventually uniting them. Mr Beebe is an ambiguous character. Urbane and sociable, he is nevertheless an ascetic man who unlike Mr Emerson has no apparent feeling for sexual passion and is in fact 'from rather profound reasons somewhat chilly in his attitude towards the other sex' (38). Thus, though he is friendly to Lucy at first, he ends by rejecting her. He is a goat in sheep's clothing.

Quite another sort of clergyman – an unadulterated goat in fact – is the Reverend Cuthbert Eager. A hypocritical snob, he mouths pieties, pontificates about art, and cultivates the society of Florence's wealthy English colony.

He knew the people who never walked about with Baedekers, who had learnt to take a siesta after lunch, who took drives the pension tourists had never heard of, and saw by private influence galleries which were closed to them. Living in delicate seclusion, some in furnished flats, others in Renaissance villas on Fiesole's slope, they read, wrote, studied, and exchanged ideas, thus attaining to that intimate knowledge, or rather perception, of Florence which is denied to all who carry in their pockets the coupons of Cook. (59)

Mr Eager contributes to Lucy's eventual muddle when he

declares to her and Charlotte that old Mr Emerson, whom he had known in London, had 'murdered his wife in the sight of God', an accusation whose true meaning is clarified only towards the end of the novel when it appears that it was Eager, not Emerson, who was responsible for the 'murder'.

A third character, and one of the best of Forster's minor ones, is Eleanor Lavish, an aging novelist of dubious talent, who is busily acquiring local colour for her next novel, a work destined to aggravate Lucy's crisis. Hearty, roguish and brisk, she springs full-blown to life when she offers, the morning after Lucy's arrival, to guide her to Santa Croce:

'I will take you by a dear dirty back way, Miss Honeychurch, and if you bring me luck, we shall have an adventure.'

Lucy said that this was most kind, and at once opened the Baedeker, to see where Santa Croce was.

'Tut, tut! Miss Lucy! I hope we shall soon emancipate you from Baedeker. He does but touch the surface of things. As to the true Italy – he does not even dream of it. The true Italy is only to be found by patient observation.'

. . . Then Miss Lavish darted under the archway of the white bullocks, and she stopped, and she cried:

'A smell! a true Florentine smell! Every city, let me teach you, has its own smell.'

'Is it a very nice smell?' said Lucy, who had inherited from her mother a distaste to dirt.

'One doesn't come to Italy for niceness,' was the retort; 'one comes for life. Buon giorno! Buon giorno!' bowing right and left. 'Look at that adorable wine-cart! How the driver stares at us, dear, simple soul!' (19–20)

Miss Lavish soon captivates the more timid Charlotte, who comes to regard her as her most intimate friend and confidante, a fact that also contributes to Lucy's crisis.

Lucy's involvement with George progresses through a series of critical encounters and episodes. The first occurs one evening shortly after her arrival when, availing herself of Charlotte's absence, she goes out into the streets alone. After buying some prints at Alinari's, she wanders into the Piazza della Signoria. She wants some excitement, and almost immediately she gets it. By the Loggia, two Italians are arguing over money. Suddenly one stabs the other, who, mortally wounded, the blood streaming down his unshaven chin, bends toward Lucy 'with a look of interest', and falls. A crowd bears him to the fountain; and Lucy faints. But just before losing consciousness, she catches a glimpse of young George Emerson who, by a typical Forsterian coincidence, happens to be a few steps away. He is looking at her, she notices, 'across' the spot where the murder had taken place. 'How very odd! Across something.' (49) The 'across' is significant. On her first evening in the pension, George had seemed to her to be smiling 'across something'. Later, meeting him in Summer Street, she bows to him 'across the rubbish that cumbers the world' (155). George, then, as the direction of his glance indicates, must help her to clear away the rubbish – the rubbish of convention in Lucy's soul that keeps her from directly experiencing life. That their first crucial encounter should take place in Florence's most celebrated square is also significant. Ever conscious of the spirit of place, Forster is generally careful to relate action to setting, and the present scene affords no exception. As the site of some of the bloodier moments in Florence's history, the Piazza is well suited to the present event. Hard and stony, it reflects a different side to Italy from the charm and warmth that Lucy has glimpsed from her pension window and during her walk with Miss Lavish. The spontaneity and passion that promote love and friendship, the novel suggests, can just as readily lead to violence and sudden death. Forster's realism embraces both the positive and negative poles of an emotional charge.

When Lucy comes to, she is on the Uffizi steps with George. He is still looking at her, but now 'not across anything', for both of them together have 'crossed some spiritual boundary'. Lucy feels that the world is suddenly 'pale and void of its original meaning'. George knows that 'something tremendous has happened', which he must face 'without getting muddled'. This 'something tremendous' is not simply the murder that they have witnessed, it is the bond of mutual sympathy, as yet only half-conscious, that their common experience has engendered.

Lucy, however, is not yet ready to forgo her world, pale and

void though it seems. Worried that word of her adventure
might reach the pension and compromise her respectability,
she tries to shake George off by sending him back to the piazza
to look for her photographs while she returns to the pension
alone. The ruse does not work. Recovering the pictures,
George insists on accompanying her, for she might, as he
implies, faint again. Together they walk toward the Arno, and,
leaning their elbows on the parapet ('There is at times,' remarks Forster, 'a magic in identity of position'), look down on
the river. Then George drops the photographs into the
swirling water. 'They were covered with blood,' he tells her in
excuse. 'I don't know; I may just mean that they frightened
me.' (51) Whatever he means, his action suggests that Lucy
must learn to accept life rather than the pallid substitute
afforded by art. Sweeping her pictures out to sea, the river
embodies a wild and inexorable natural force that Lucy can
only oppose at her peril.

Yet oppose it she does. Offering the pension a suitably
abridged account of what has occurred, she sows the seeds of
muddle. The next crucial incident occurs a few days later
when, despite her wish to avoid another encounter with
George, she finds herself joining him on an outing to Fiesole.
A Jane-Austenish party and a fine example of Forster's gift
for social comedy, the outing seems from the start to be
presided over by Pan. Planned by Mr Eager as a 'partie carée'
to include himself, Mr Beebe, Lucy and Charlotte and to
feature tea at a Renaissance villa, it is thrown off balance when
Mr Beebe, without consulting Mr Eager, invites the two Emersons and Miss Lavish to join them. Not only is tea at the villa
now out of the question, two carriages rather than one must
be hired to take the party to Fiesole. The group, furthermore,
is thoroughly ill-sorted. Not only is Lucy anxious to avoid
George, but Mr Eager does not like Mr Emerson or Miss
Lavish. The ensuing conflict and comedy are heightened
when, much to Mr Eager's annoyance and Mr Emerson's
delight, the driver of Lucy's carriage makes love to his girl. At
the summit the party, which has never been unified, splits into

three groups, with Lucy, still trying to avoid George, joining Miss Lavish and Charlotte. But the two women, now intimate, do not want Lucy around, and soon find a chance to send her off to look for the two ministers. Not knowing the Italian for 'ministers' Lucy asks the amorous cab-driver the whereabouts of the 'good men' ('i buoni uomini'); and he, with romantic perversity, leads her to a violet-strewn terrace commanding a magnificent view of the Val d'Arno. Enchanted she sinks to the ground to see, standing above her, a good man. 'But he was not the good man that she had expected, and he was alone.' (80) As the cab-driver enjoins her to show 'courage and love', George bends down and kisses her. But even as he does so, the lyrical moment is shattered by the cry of 'Lucy! Lucy! Lucy!' Miss Bartlett is standing 'brown against the view'.

The Fiesole outing, culminating in George's kiss and Charlotte's intrusion, forms the climax of the first part of the novel. Lucy, thoroughly alarmed by what has occurred, accedes to Charlotte's proposal that they leave the next morning for Rome to join friends of the Honeychurches, Mrs Vyse and her son Cecil; and thus, for the time being, she is able to escape the consequences of her involvement.

The scene between Lucy and Charlotte, upon their return from Fiesole, is a masterpiece of ironic comedy and psychological penetration. Feeling the weight of her inexperience and the superior wisdom of Charlotte, Lucy expresses a sorrow for what has happened and a warmth for her cousin that belie her deeper feelings. Charlotte, for her part, is anxious enough to preserve her reputation as a reliable chaperon with Lucy's mother, whose money has made the trip possible, to capitalize on Lucy's immediate need for understanding and love. At the same time, as an unloved and sexually chilly spinster, she is not above gaining a vicarious warmth by raking over the coals of Lucy's adventure:

'You are so young and inexperienced, you have lived among such nice people, that you cannot realize what men can be – how they can take a brutal pleasure in insulting a woman whom her sex does not protect and rally round. This afternoon, for example, if I had not arrived, what would have happened?'

'I can't think,' said Lucy gravely.

Something in her voice made Miss Bartlett repeat her question, intoning it more vigorously.

'What would have happened if I hadn't arrived?'

'I can't think,' said Lucy again.

'When he insulted you, how would you have replied?'

'I hadn't time to think. You came.'

'Yes, but won't you tell me now what you would have done?' (88)

How penetratingly the following passage reveals the mixture of moral blindness, self-solicitude and craft governing the conduct of each woman toward the other:

They began to sort their clothes for packing, for there was no time to lose, if they were to catch the train to Rome. Lucy, when admonished, began to move to and fro between the rooms, more conscious of the discomforts of packing by candle-light than of a subtler ill. Charlotte, who was practical without ability, knelt by the side of an empty trunk, vainly endeavouring to pave it with books of varying thickness and size. She gave two or three sighs, for the stooping posture hurt her back, and, for all her diplomacy, she felt that she was growing old. The girl heard her as she entered the room, and was seized with one of those emotional impulses to which she could never attribute a cause. She only felt that the candle would burn better, the packing go easier, the world be happier, if she could give and receive some human love. The impulse had come before to-day, but never so strongly. She knelt down by her cousin's side and took her in her arms.

Miss Bartlett returned the embrace with tenderness and warmth. But she was not a stupid woman, and she knew perfectly well that Lucy did not love her, but needed her to love. For it was in ominous tones that she said, after a long pause:

'Dearest Lucy, how will you ever forgive me?'

Lucy was on her guard at once, knowing by bitter experience what forgiving Miss Bartlett meant. Her emotion relaxed, she modified her embrace a little, and she said:

'Charlotte dear, what do you mean? As if I have anything to forgive!' (90)

More persuasively than by any overt assertion, the scene shows how much the two women have in common. Both are too bound by the conventions of their class, by the conventions governing the behaviour of a lady, to give themselves fearlessly to life. Repressing a need for love and spiritual freedom, both women inevitably become hypocrites. Lucy, being younger, is more resilient; she has the capacity to grow and might yet be saved. Charlotte, on the other hand, is spiritually moribund.

For too long she has been, in Forster's words, with 'the vast armies of the benighted, who follow neither the heart nor the brain, and march to their destiny by catch-words' (204).

The second part of the novel finds Lucy back home at Windy Corner, some three months later, with her mother, her brother Freddy, and Cecil Vyse, to whom she is about to become engaged. With Italy, as she hopes, behind her, she is ready to make a respectable marriage with a man whom, as is patently evident, she does not love. Cecil is the antithesis of George. Where George is supposedly natural, Cecil is 'mediaeval', a word that applies both to his appearance and outlook. Tall and ascetic-looking, he recalls those 'fastidious saints who guard the portals of a French cathedral' (100). And his attitude to Lucy is equally 'mediaeval', for he regards her not as an autonomous human being with a life of her own but as a treasure to be protected, a work of art through which he discerns some ultimate and ineffable beauty:

Italy worked some marvel in her. It gave her light, and – which he held more precious – it gave her shadow. Soon he detected in her a wonderful reticence. She was like a woman of Leonardo da Vinci's, whom we love not so much for herself as for the things that she will not tell us. The things are assuredly not of this life...(101–2)

He reminds one a bit of Philip Herriton, and of some of the young Cambridge aesthetes of Forster's time, men like Lytton Strachey and Duncan Grant who, according to Bertrand Russell, 'did not seek to preserve any kinship with the Philistine', but 'aimed rather at a life of retirement among fine shades and nice feelings, and conceived of the good as consisting in the passionate mutual admirations of a clique of the elite'.[2] There is in him too a detachment toward people similar to that which Forster found in Dante in his early essay on the Italian poet.[3] Just as Dante, according to Forster, looked through Beatrice and saw God, so Cecil looks through Lucy and sees, if not God, at least a premonition of ultimate beauty. In Cecil,

[2] Michael Holroyd, *Lytton Strachey*, p. 207. New York, 1968.
[3] 'Dante', *The Working Men's College Journal*, vol. 10 (February–April 1908). Reprinted in *Albergo Empedocle and Other Writings*, ed. G. H. Thomson (New York, 1971).

finally, as in Philip Herriton, one discerns an aspect of Forster himself – of his recurring detachment and exaltation of art and beauty, a side of him radically opposed to his love of people and the life of experience.[4]

Lucy, then, tries to commit herself to Cecil and his 'medi-aeval' ideals of womanhood. She also tries to commit herself to Summer Street; and since Cecil, who is from London, looks down on Summer Street, the double attempt simply com-pounds her muddle. But the problem confronting her, as Forster presents it, is by no means simple. It appears, for instance, to be less simple and clear-cut than Rickie Elliot's problem of whether to cut himself free of a bad marriage and a bad school. Cecil may be a snob, but he is not stupid and not lacking in dignity. And Summer Street, partly because it is a provincial village, affords a pleasant life to those who belong to it. Forster's sympathy with its spirit emerges in the contrast he draws between Summer Street and the London world of the Vyses. Mrs Honeychurch, for example, although limited in her sympathies by her class and intelligence, is a warm-hearted woman whose love for her home and children is genuine and unstinting. But Mrs Vyse has been

swamped by London, for it needs a strong head to live among many people. The too vast orb of her fate had crushed her; and she had seen too many seasons, too many cities, too many men, for her abilities, and even with Cecil she was mechanical, and behaved as if he was not one son, but, so to speak, a filial crowd. (140–1)

Freddy, Lucy's brother, is lively and natural; Cecil, on the other hand, a product of London, is languid and artificial. And finally, to cap Summer Street's superiority over London, there is the view of the Sussex Weald, which Forster obviously loves as much as Lucy and which certainly rivals that of the Val d'Arno from Fiesole. Cecil sneers at Windy Corner and Summer Street, but fails to see that 'Lucy had consecrated her environment by the thousand little civilities that create a ten-

4 See 'The Art of Fiction', interview of E. M. Forster by P. N. Furbank and F. J. H. Haskell in *Paris Review*, vol. 1 (Spring 1953), 28–41, esp. 33, for Forster's admission that both characters are partly self-portraits.

derness in time, and that though her eyes saw its defects, her heart refused to despise it entirely.' (127)

Yet difficult as her choice is, it is clear that Lucy is choosing badly. She is choosing, in effect, to remain a child, to hold on to a 'view' that, thanks to Florence, is no longer relevant to her needs. Her condition recalls Rickie Elliot's when he tried to forget Stephen. Like Rickie, she enters a 'cloud of unreality;' and no more than he, can she be allowed to remain in this condition.

As in *The Longest Journey* Forster reintroduces his saviour by means of a far-fetched coincidence, thereby implying that Lucy's salvation will depend at least as much on good luck as on her own character. Ironically, the agent of her good luck is Cecil himself, who happens to run into the Emersons, whom he has never met or even heard of, in the National Gallery, and, upon learning that they need a house, suggests that they rent a small villa in Summer Street belonging to a friend of the Honeychurches, Sir Harry Otway. In making the suggestion, Cecil is prompted by a somewhat Meredithean sense of comedy. Having heard Sir Harry bemoan his inability to find desirable tenants for his house, Cecil considers him a complete snob and would like to teach him – and Summer Street – a lesson. The Emersons, who are obviously uncultured, are ideal for his purpose. In the meantime, Lucy has suggested as tenants two elderly spinsters, the Miss Alans, whom she met at the pension in Florence, and has received Sir Harry's permission to write to them. But the fact carries no weight with Cecil, nor with Sir Harry. The latter accepts the Emersons, and before Lucy is aware of the fact, they have moved in.

From now on everything conspires against Lucy's attempt to forget her past. First comes a letter from Charlotte reversing her original advice that Lucy say nothing about George to her mother. Now, it seems, she should tell her everything, for Eleanor Lavish had run into George in Summer Street and told him that Lucy lived there. Charlotte has an additional reason, as it turns out, for advising Lucy to 'make a clean breast' of everything; but this Lucy has yet to learn and sees no reason to make a family confession.

Her meeting with George now virtually assured, it only remains for Forster to stage it. This he does in a scene both comic and allegoric. Freddy and Mr Beebe, who have just introduced themselves to the Emersons, take George for a swim in the Sacred Lake, a nearby pond. Forster's account of the three men splashing and swimming and united in friendship by their common activity recalls Lawrence. Like his younger contemporary, Forster stresses the liberating and spiritual value of the experience. It is 'a call to the blood and to the relaxed will, a passing benediction...a holiness, a spell' (153). But unlike Lawrence, Forster also sees its absurdity, the sheer fun of the thing. The picture of the three 'gentlemen' rotating breast-high in the pond 'after the fashion of the nymphs in Götterdammerung', and of Freddy and George racing around in Mr Beebe's clerical garb injects a note of hilarity quite unlike the more sustained and apocalyptic mood in a comparable scene of Lawrence's. The same sense of absurdity colours the unexpected intrusion of Lucy, Mrs Honeychurch and Cecil on their way through the woods to visit a neighbour:

Barefoot, barechested, radiant and personable against the shadowy woods, he called:
  'Hullo, Miss Honeychurch! Hullo!'
  'Bow, Lucy; better bow. Whoever is it? I shall bow.'
Miss Honeychurch bowed. (153)

The woodland meeting, of course, is only a preamble to further encounters. The crucial one occurs on a Sunday afternoon at Windy Corner where George has been invited to play tennis. He plays enthusiastically and with a desire to win, a fact that draws Lucy to him in spite of herself as she contrasts his spirit with Cecil's languid air of superiority. During a lull in the game, she looks at the back of George's head. 'She did not want to stroke it, but she saw herself wanting to stroke it; the sensation was curious.' (184) The crisis comes when Cecil insists on reading them a scene from a novel.

It is none other than Eleanor Lavish's *Under a Loggia* and contains, at the beginning of chapter 2, as Lucy hears to her horror, a thinly fictitious account of her moment with George on the terrace in Fiesole. Charlotte, as she will soon confess (for she is a guest at Windy Corner), has confided the entire incident to her friend. Now Lucy can only try to stop the reading. And so she suggests tea. But as they file in to the house and Cecil returns to fetch the novel, George, never a laggard when opportunity offers, blunders against her on the narrow path and, for the second time in her life, kisses her.

His action brings the crisis to a head. That he must go seems evident to Lucy. She is engaged to Cecil and is determined to go through with it, to go through, that is, with the respectable lie rather than face the difficult truth. Having extracted from Charlotte a tremulous confession of guilt, she goes with her into the dining room to confront George. She confronts him directly, without preamble: 'I can't have it, Mr Emerson. I cannot even talk to you. Go out of this house, and never come into it again as long as I live here.' (193) But once again George refuses to act according to expectation or formula, and calmly proceeds to catalogue Cecil's inadequacies – his snobbery, meanness, puritanism, and his proprietary regard for women. Ignoring his outstretched arms and his plea that she marry him, Lucy sends him away. But his words have impressed her. That evening she breaks her engagement with Cecil. The immediate cause of her decision was her hearing his patronizing refusal to join Freddy for tennis, but the deeper cause is her knowledge that George is right. And when she tells Cecil that he too must go, she echoes in her defence the very words that George had spoken against him. 'You're the sort who can't know any one intimately...you wrap yourself up in art and books and music, and would try to wrap up me.' (201)

Yet for all her knowledge that George was right that she cannot love Cecil, she is not yet ready to face the whole truth. Her dismissal of both young men involves her in a series of lies that screen the truth from herself as well as from those around her. To George she has asserted that she loves Cecil and not him, and to Cecil that she loves no one. To her family and Mr Beebe – now rector at Summer Street – she pretends that her rupture with Cecil was solely due to his dominating character, his inability to 'let a woman decide for herself' (214).

She gets a chance, as she feels, to escape from the whole mess when she learns that the Miss Alans are going to Greece. She will go with them. Charlotte, anxious to clamp the lid on a pot still threatening to bubble over, encourages her to go and manages to persuade Mr Beebe that another trip abroad would be the best thing for Lucy to tide her over the 'shock' of her broken engagement. But before she can leave, she has an eleventh-hour meeting with old Mr Emerson – a meeting that seems fortuitous but that Charlotte, inwardly sympathetic, for all her prim demeanour, with Lucy's predicament, has helped to arrange. He and George have closed up house and are about to move to London, for George, according to his father, has 'gone under': he cannot bear to remain in Summer Street any longer. Saying nothing about her broken engagement, Lucy urges him to stay, telling him that she is going to Greece – with Cecil, as she implies and as Mr Emerson naturally assumes. But when Mr Beebe, who breaks in on the meeting, makes it clear that Lucy is going with the two Miss Alans and not with Cecil, Mr Emerson sees at once to the heart of the muddle. 'You love George . . . you love the boy body and soul, plainly, directly, as he loves you, and no other word expresses it. You won't marry the other man for his sake.' (237) Breaking into tears, Lucy admits the truth. Mr Beebe, however, is disappointed – chiefly, it appears, by the fact that George has decided to marry. 'Marry George, Miss Honeychurch,' he advises with some asperity. 'He will do admirably.' But Mr Emerson kisses her and gives her strength and a sense of 'deities reconciled'.

Thus Lucy attains a feeling not unlike that of Margaret Schlegel in *Howards End* that the needs of her inner life have finally been harmonized with the demands of the outer. Her universe comes to fit. It is all of a piece. One should beware, nevertheless, of reading into this resolution of Lucy's muddle

a resolution of Forster's own effort to convey the multifarious-
ness of life through the unifying vision of art. Lucy after all
has only '*a sense* of deities reconciled'. Mr Emerson can give
her strength, he cannot give her ultimate vision. It is only '*as
if*' he has made her see 'the whole of everything at once' (240).
In the final chapter, which follows, George and Lucy are honey-
mooning at their old pension in Florence. George is completely
happy. His nagging doubts as to the ultimate purpose of life
have been resolved. As Alan Wilde has observed, his Everlasting Why has turned into an Everlasting Yes. And one must
agree, it seems to me, with Wilde's assertion that 'the problems
that George himself raises' are not 'adequately answered by
his love for Lucy'.[5] Lucy's happiness, on the other hand, is
adulterated with a sense that she has alienated her family and
Mr Beebe 'perhaps forever'. Her mother and brother are too
'disgusted at her past hypocrisy' to forgive her marriage to
George; Mr Beebe, for all his tolerance and insight, is blind
to the virtue of sexual passion. Obviously, then, Lucy has not
really succeeded in reconciling her deities. The god who presides over Windy Corner and Summer Street remains implac-
able. Surely, she declares, 'if we act the truth, the people who
really love us are sure to come back to us in the long run' (244).
But George is not convinced, and his laconic 'perhaps' would
seem to reflect Forster's characteristic tentativeness. Perhaps
we can both save our souls and have the world. Perhaps
private truth and public fact can be reconciled. The only
present certainties are the happiness of the lovers and the
inevitability of natural process, of age giving way to youth, of
youth to maturity, and maturity to age. The final 'song' that
the lovers hear is that of the Arno 'bearing down the snows
of winter into the Mediterranean' (246).

Thus, although the novel's ending is generally and rightly
considered happy, Lucy's happiness is qualified by her knowledge that she has alienated her family. Her salvation, moreover, is shot through with moral ambiguity, for it has
depended less on her own virtue than on good luck and the

---

[5] Alan Wilde, *Art and Order, A Study of E. M. Forster*, p. 60. New York, 1964.

influence of others. Her presence and George's in the piazza at the time of the murder, her encounter with George in Fiesole and Charlotte's unexpected intrusion into the scene, the Emersons' meeting with Cecil in the National Gallery and their consequent move to Summer Street, Cecil's reading of Miss Lavish's novel, and Lucy's eleventh-hour meeting with Mr Emerson – these and other events show that Lucy is caught in a network of forces, all of them contributing to her final happiness and over which she has little or no control. That she is saved and Charlotte damned has less to do with the respective virtue of the two women (and Forster, as we have seen, underscores their similar timid conventionalism) than with the fact that Lucy is younger and luckier. Upon the return from Fiesole, she and her companions narrowly missed being struck by lightening. That they were not was the merest good fortune. Life, the novel suggests, is a precarious business, and the forces that sustain it or blight it are largely external to the individual.

The moral ambiguity of Lucy's experience and the implication that man is subject to external, and sometimes mysterious, cosmic forces, is further sustained through the novel's pervasive imagery of light and darkness. Light, whose source is the sun, signifies clarity, honesty and truth; darkness, the absence of sunlight, signifies the reverse. The sunlight that shines on Windy Corner and Summer Street at the beginning of the second part of the novel conveys the warmth and clarity that Lucy needs. It is solar light, to be sure; but it is also, Forster implies, the celestial light of childhood:

The drawing-room curtains at Windy Corner had been pulled to meet, for the carpet was new and deserved protection from the August sun. They were heavy curtains, reaching almost to the ground, and the light that filtered through them was subdued and varied. A poet – none was present – might have quoted, 'Life like a dome of many-coloured glass,' or might have compared the curtains to sluice-gates, lowered against the intolerable tides of heaven. Without was poured a sea of radiance; within, the glory, though visible, was tempered to the capacities of man. (94)

Lunching with her mother and brother, Lucy feels herself to be in a timeless world. 'Her mother would always sit there, her brother here. The sun, though it had moved a little since the morning, would never be hidden behind the western hills.' (180) Yet in no other of Forster's novels is time and change so insisted upon. Spring gives way to summer, summer to fall, fair weather to foul; the river that bears Lucy's photographs to the sea also bears 'the snows of winter into the Mediterranean'; the sun, for all Lucy's wish to the contrary, moves inexorably across the sky. Even as she tries to hold on to her childhood, 'summer was ending' and the earth 'hastening to re-enter darkness' (196–7). And the darkness, Forster implies, is moral as well as natural. The bad weather that marks the breaking-up of summer has a metaphysical dimension:

Grey clouds were charging across tissues of white, which stretched and shredded and tore slowly, until through their final layers there gleamed a hint of the disappearing blue. Summer was retreating. The wind roared, the trees groaned, yet the noise seemed insufficient for those vast operations in heaven. The weather was breaking up, breaking, broken, and it is a sense of the fit rather than of the supernatural that equips such crises with the salvos of angelic artillery. Mr Beebe's eyes rested on Windy Corner, where Lucy sat, practising Mozart. No smile came to his lips, and, changing the subject again, he said: 'We shan't have rain, but we shall have darkness, so let us hurry on. The darkness last night was appalling.' (216)

The implication of Mr Beebe's quasi-apocalyptic utterance goes far beyond Lucy's personal predicament: it points to some malignant force in the universe itself that threatens the safety of us all. Lucy, it is suggested, is but a pawn in some inscrutable cosmic process. Facing the darkness of her own soul, she fears 'that king of terrors – light' (225). George, on the other hand, fearing the darkness, wants to stand in the sunlight. But sunlight, as he recognizes, engenders shadow. 'We cast a shadow on something wherever we stand, and it is no good moving from place to place to save things; because the shadow always follows.' (176) Good and evil, clarity and muddle, in other words, are inherent in the nature of things. Light implies darkness, darkness light. The thought here recalls Godbole's assertion in *A Passage to India* that good and evil express 'the whole universe...they are both of them aspects of my Lord.

He is present in the one, absent in the other... Yet absence implies presence.'[6]

The moral ambiguity – the mixture of light and darkness – that can surround an event is nowhere more pointedly shown than in the scene in the piazza where Lucy witnesses the murder. Coming into the square, she sees it in shadow. The figure of Neptune is 'unsubstantial in the twilight', the Loggia shows like a cave, its statues 'shadowy but immortal'. It is the hour, Forster remarks, 'of unreality'. Only upon the tower of the palazzo does the sun still shine. Suggestive of Lucy's still unexpressed sexual yearnings, it seems 'no longer a tower, no longer supported by earth, but some unattainable treasure throbbing in the tranquil sky. Its brightness mesmerized her...' (48) The pattern of light and shade is emblematic of the ensuing event – of a passionate outburst leading to the death of one human being and the salvation of two others.

A Room with a View is a tightly controlled book, and one of the ways in which Forster shows his control is in his careful deployment of 'views'. Key characters can be measured by the kinds of views they respond to. Indeed the ability to respond to views at all separates the saveable from the damned; for only those who respond to some kind of view, the novel suggests, are able to love. The views that Lucy responds to in Florence and from the terrace at Windy Corner are vital and natural; they are scenic reminders of the course that she must follow. Cecil, on the other hand, chiefly responds to art. Conceiving Lucy as a work of art, he views her in his mind against a Leonardo-like background of flower-clad mountains and shadowy rocks (102). His views are aesthetic and clearly to be connected with his indifference to people and dislike of sport. Lucy connects George with the view from Fiesole, but Cecil she can only connect with a viewless drawing-room (122). Charlotte, loveless and self-encased, responds to no views at all. Entering her room at the pension, she immediately fastens the shutters (15); and staying at Windy Corner, she begs to

[6] *A Passage to India*, 178. Harcourt, Brace, New York, 1952.

be given 'an inferior spare room – something with no view, anything' (164). When she intrudes on Lucy and George at Fiesole, it is entirely in keeping with her nature that she should block the view; her very presence, in fact, gives Lucy 'the sensation of a fog' (15). Finally, in complete contrast to Charlotte, the Emersons respond most intensely to views of the open sky, for like their famous American namesake they are transcendentally-minded. 'My father,' remarks George approvingly, 'says that there is only one perfect view – the view of the sky straight over our heads, and that all these views on earth are but bungled copies of it.' (184) Taken together the novel's 'views' serve to enforce its theme and structure and to provide a measure of character.

Forster's third novel, then, is a romantic one, concerned with a simpler, more conventional society than our own. But its romance and outmoded conventionalism need not blind one to the fact that it also explores with subtlety and intelligence a perennial problem: the difficulty of being true to oneself and to others in a precarious world largely governed by chance – a world in which good and bad, clarity and muddle, violence and love are inextricably intertwined and as much a part of the nature of things as time and change themselves. Forster's next novel, *Howards End*, is broader in focus and more ambitious; but it is less tightly controlled and less satisfying.

5

Howards End

Howards End, Forster's fourth novel, has a wider social range than his previous fiction. In addition to the society of the cultivated and well-to-do, it deals with the world of business and that of shabby gentility. Lionel Trilling declares that it concerns England's fate;[1] but it does not, for it leaves too much of England out of account. It has nothing to say of the very poor, who, like the starving millions of India, drift beyond Forster's 'educated vision'. Nor does it foresee the social changes that war will bring, or England's decline as a great power.

No, it belongs to a quieter, more intimate world than the England of 1910, much less that of today. It is a predominantly upper-middle-class world, with town houses and country houses for the well-to-do, and plenty of servants; a world where class distinctions are taken for granted (people still refer to the 'lower orders'), and a motor car on a country road is anomalous enough to be viewed with alarm, like military tanks on a residential street today. In the world of the novel, the British Empire is in its heyday, business and commerce thrive, the poor, as far as possible, are kept in their place, and gentlemen try to protect ladies from the grosser realities of life.

Nevertheless, in one important respect, the world of *Howards End* does resemble our own: socially and spiritually it is fragmented. Except in their formal dealings, the various classes of society scarcely communicate with one another. There is a gulf between rich and poor, and a subtler, but nonetheless insidious one, between men and women. Public life is divorced from private, the outer world from the inner.

What role can such a world provide those who deeply care

[1] Lionel Trilling, *E. M. Forster*, p. 118. Norfolk, Conn., 1943.

for the inner life? Must they, so far as possible, cut themselves off from the outer one, or can they vitally connect themselves with it? The question, which is of fundamental importance to Forster as a humanist and a liberal, underlies *Howards End*. The novel embodies a search for an answer.

Forster's fictive imagination tends to work allegorically, and nowhere more obviously so than in *Howards End*. The novel's world is composed of contraries – of antithetical places and people, embodying antithetical values. There is the city, London, and the country, mainly Hertfordshire. The city, we are told, is 'Satanic', a vast congeries of streets and buildings, in which the coming and going of people is largely determined by the impersonal forces of business and commerce. A place of flux and change, not unlike Eliot's 'Unreal city, under the brown fog', it gives rise to our modern 'civilization of luggage'. There is no community in the city; only propinquity.

The country, in contrast, fosters community. It is settled, peaceful, harmonious, its life following the rhythm of seasonal change and anchored to the earth. It is the old England, now threatened with extinction. Hilton, the village adjoining Howards End, is fast becoming what we today call a commuter town, its railway station striking 'an indeterminate note. Into what country will it lead, England or Suburbia?' (A13; K20)[2] Looking out at the country from Howards End, Helen Schlegel notes the brown haze of London on the horizon. 'You see that in Surrey and even Hampshire now...And London is only part of something else, I'm afraid. Life's going to be melted down, all over the world.' (A337; K388-9)

Just as the country is opposed to the city, so are the major characters to one another. Margaret and Helen Schlegel value the inner life. The Wilcox family with the notable exception of Ruth Wilcox, values the outer. Independently rich, Margaret and Helen Schlegel live with their adolescent brother Tibby in Wickham Place, a comfortable London house on a quiet street, the two young women (Helen is twenty-one when

---

[2] Page references in *Howards End* are from the Abinger edition, 1973 (A) and the Knopf edition, 1946 (K).

the novel opens, Margaret twenty-nine) devoting most of their energy to conversation and culture. Henry Wilcox, a successful London businessman, lives with his wife Ruth and their three grown children at Howards End, Ruth's ancestral home. Showing little interest in casual conversation and culture, Henry and the children prefer to devote their spare energy to calisthenics and outdoor games. The Schlegels are half-German;[3] the Wilcoxes all-English. The Schlegel household is dominated by a feminine spirit; the Wilcox, by a masculine one.

Superficially Margaret and Helen are similar, both being liberal, cultivated, intelligent, and, compared to almost any modern girl of their class, unbelievably sheltered and ignorant of the world. Yet the antitheses that help to define the novel's structure also distinguish Helen from Margaret.

Helen, the younger and prettier of the two, is the more impressionable and impulsive. Visiting Howards End for the first time, she precipitately becomes infatuated not only with Paul, the younger son, but with the entire Wilcox family, so refreshingly different, as she feels, from her own. One kiss from Paul under the wych-elm is enough to bring about their engagement. But the engagement is off the next day when Helen is overwhelmed to discover that Paul lacks the courage to announce the fact to his family. Disillusioned, she now sees them as 'a fraud, just a wall of newspapers and motor-cars and golf-clubs', behind which lie 'panic and emptiness' (A23; K32). Helen is a romantic idealist. Truth and justice, she believes, are absolute, and she finds it hard to compromise with the world as it is. Long after the episode with Paul, she takes up the cause of Leonard Bast, the young clerk, who loses his job largely, as Helen feels, through the misadvice of Henry Wilcox. Helen's attempt to solve Leonard's problem is consistent with her extremism. Bringing him and his blowsy wife Jacky uninvited to Henry's daughter's wedding-party, she tries to trap Henry into giving him a job. But the project misfires when Jacky recognises Henry to be her former lover and

---

[3] A cancelled passage in the MS of *Howards End*, at King's College, Cambridge, refers to the Schlegels' father as 'a distant relation of the great critic'.

accosts him with the fact. That night at the local inn, Helen and Leonard copulate, and Helen becomes pregnant. The affair seems farfetched, although it accords with Leonard's need for sympathy and Helen's earlier romance with Paul. Neither man did she really love. Both to her were symbols, Paul of romantic virility, Leonard of the poor and exploited. 'Did Leonard,' she wonders, 'grow out of Paul?' (A310; K359) The answer, obviously, is yes.

Helen's temperament is revealed in one of the novel's most memorable scenes, that of the concert in Queen's Hall. Listening to Beethoven's Fifth Symphony, Helen absorbs the music not as music, but as an inspiring and terrifying sonic phantasmagoria: 'heroes and shipwrecks' in the first movement, 'goblins' proclaiming 'Panic and emptiness!' in the Scherzo, and 'gusts of splendour, the heroism, the youth, the magnificence of life and of death' in the Finale. Her response recalls Rickie Elliot's to the sight of Agnes and Gerald kissing, when he suddenly feels himself to be gazing at coloured valleys and pinnacles of virgin snow and to be hearing 'a fragment of the Tune of tunes';[4] and, in fact, Rickie and Helen have much in common. The music projects Helen's fears and aspirations. A would-be heroine, she called up psychological goblins when she fell for Paul and discerned in the Wilcoxes 'panic and emptiness'.

Her response to the symphony also foreshadows much of the action. Leonard and his umbrella are a 'goblin footfall' issuing from the abyss. Throughout the novel, goblins continue to rise, and panic and emptiness to resound. In taking up Leonard's cause, Helen tries, in effect, to behave heroically, and she is nearly 'shipwrecked'. Following her one-night affair with Leonard, she turns up at Tibby's in Oxford, wearing 'the look of a sailor who has lost everything at sea' (A247; K286).

Margaret, too, is impulsive, but less so than Helen, and much more balanced in outlook. Whereas Helen declares an exclusive commitment to the inner life ('I know that personal relations are the real life, for ever and ever' (A25; K34),

---

[4] *The Longest Journey*, 52. New Directions, Norfolk, Conn.

Margaret sees that the outer life also has claims. 'The truth is,' she tells Helen,

'that there is a great outer life that you and I have never touched – a life in which telegrams and anger count. Personal relations, that we think supreme, are not supreme there. There love means marriage settlements, death, death duties. So far I'm clear. But here's my difficulty. This outer life, though obviously horrid, often seems the real one – there's grit in it. It does breed character. Do personal relations lead to sloppiness in the end?' (A25; K33)

More keenly than Helen, she sees the extent to which their comfortable, cultivated existence is tied to business by an economic umbilical cord. 'I stand each year upon six hundred pounds, and Helen upon the same, and Tibby will stand upon eight, and as fast as our pounds crumble way into the sea they are renewed – from the sea, yes, from the sea. And all our thoughts are the thoughts of six-hundred-pounders, and all our speeches.' (A59; K71–2) By what justification, then, she wonders, do she, Helen, and Tibby seal themselves off from the outer life? Not only did their forebears earn the money on which they live, but that money is invested in business shares.

But her regard for the outer life is prompted by more than a sense of economic responsibility. It also contains an emotional, even, perhaps, a sexual, element. Sheltered, inhibited, and yet curious, like an Ibsen heroine, Margaret is simultaneously repelled by the masculine world of business and attracted to it. On the one hand, it is 'obviously horrid'; on the other, it somehow seems 'real'. Business people like the Wilcoxes get things done; they are virile and strong, and their household would seem to complement the too-feminine character of her own. 'Ours is a female house,' she declares, with a touch of regret. Howards End is 'irrevocably masculine' (A41; K51, 52).

Margaret, who would like to connect her life with the 'outer life', is the novel's heroine and, to a great extent, Forster's surrogate. Forster is sympathetic to Helen too: she projects, as does Rickie Elliot, his romantic and visionary strain; but it is Margaret who elicits his fullest sympathy. Like her, he is discomforted by a world in which spiritual values seem forced to exist subterraneously, cut off from the great public life around. Like her, Forster would probably prefer a world wherein unity embraces variety and public life mirrors 'whatever is good in the life within' (A25; K34). Throughout the novel, Margaret is often the mouthpiece for Forster's views.

Margaret's attempt to connect her inner life with the outer, which constitutes the novel's central action, will require of her three qualities: experience, love, and a sense of proportion. Obviously in order to assimilate the outer life, she must first experience it; otherwise she will remain, as it were, an armchair theorist whose prescription for living a fuller life has never been tested by fact. But more than experiencing it, she must come to love it, or love, at any rate, some human embodiment of its spirit, for without love no true assimilation is possible. Finally, if she is to reconcile the claims of public and private life, she must maintain a sense of proportion. But 'don't *begin* with proportion,' she tells Mrs Wilcox. 'Only prigs do that. Let proportion come in as a last resource, when the better things have failed...' (A70; K85)[5]

Both sisters reflect strains in Forster himself, and perhaps for that reason he can delineate them with insight and sympathy. Less can be said for his treatment of Henry Wilcox and his three children. Conceived as antithetical to the Schlegels, they are types rather than individuals, and types, it must be said, that would tax the credulity of a child and the sympathy of a saint.

Henry is the novel's chief flaw. A caricature of a businessman, he is stiff, easily muddled, utterly imperceptive about himself and others, and without a grain of redeeming wit and

---

[5] Proportion is an aesthetic as well as a moral value, and Margaret's feeling for it partly projects Forster's belief that art, his own included, should be ordered and balanced, though never at the expense of life. Cf. his defence of the 'Temple' section of *A Passage to India* as 'architecturally necessary' (P. N. Furbank and F. J. H. Haskell, 'The Art of Fiction', *Paris Review*, vol. 1 (spring 1953), 28), and his condemnation of James's alleged premise 'that most of human life has to disappear before he can do us a novel' (E. M. Forster, *Aspects of the Novel*, Abinger Edition, ed. O. Stallybrass, p. 109. London, 1974).

humour. Forster's dislike for the man comes through again and again. We learn of Henry's 'Olympian laugh' (153), his 'patronizing tone', and his feeling that 'what he did not know could not be worth knowing' (A129; K151). 'As is Man to the Universe,' remarks Forster, 'so was the mind of Mr Wilcox to the minds of some men – a concentrated light upon a tiny spot, a little Ten Minutes moving self-contained through its appointed years.' (A245; K284) When Henry stands exposed of having, during his first marriage, harboured a mistress and of nevertheless being unable to show charity to Helen, pregnant with Leonard's child, Forster's contempt, through his mouthpiece Margaret, reaches its height:

'Stupid, hypocritical, cruel – oh, contemptible! – a man who insults his wife when she's alive and cants with her memory when she's dead. A man who ruins a woman for his pleasure, and casts her off to ruin other men. And gives bad financial advice, and then says he is not responsible. These, man, are you. You can't recognize them, because you cannot connect. I've had enough of your unweeded kindness. I've spoilt you long enough. All your life you have been spoiled. Mrs Wilcox spoiled you. No one has ever told what you are – muddled, criminally muddled. Men like you use repentance as a blind, so don't repent. Only say to yourself, "What Helen has done, I've done."' (A305; K352–3)

If this is the outer life, the reader may wonder, why on earth should Margaret want to attach herself to it?

Forster is obviously uneasy about his treatment of Henry, and tries to humanize him by hinting at nobler traits. We hear of his charm (A129; K151), kindness (A283; K327), and strength of character (A89, 139; K105, 163 & *passim*), but the qualities are asserted rather than demonstrated. 'Some day,' we are told, 'in the millennium, there may be no need for his type. At present, homage is due to it from those who think themselves superior, and who possibly are.' (A158–9; K185) Henry is symptomatic of Forster's inability to reconcile the novel's allegorical element with its attempt to achieve social and psychological realism. Like Helen, he sees him not as a human being but a symbol: Henry is the exploiting imperialist, who, though he contributes to England's prosperity and maintains the plumbing at Howards End, is helping to turn cities into commercial nightmares populated by Leonard Basts. His children are chips from the same block.

Only Ruth Wilcox stands out from the rest of the family. One of Forster's wise old women, she incarnates the spirit of Howards End. An enigmatic, quasi-symbolic figure, less developed than Mrs Moore, whom she somewhat resembles, she values the past and the unseen, is intuitive rather than intellectual, and illustrates, by virtue of her successful marriage to Henry, the possibility of integrating past and present, the inner life and the outer. Forster professes puzzlement over her aims and attitudes ('perhaps her friendship with Margaret began at Speyer', perhaps she found Margaret more sympathetic than Helen, 'Mrs Wilcox has left few clear indications behind her' (A62; K75)), and asserts her greatness of spirit (A19–20, 21; K28, 29) but does not convey it. In fact, without his supporting commentary, she would seem unimpressive. Having discerned in Maraget her spiritual heir and bequeathed Howards End and, by implication, her husband to her, Ruth Wilcox fulfills her novelistic role and dies. But like Mrs Moore, she maintains a posthumous existence, her presence being felt, among other ways, through the character of Miss Avery, the old caretaker, who, professing to mistake Margaret for Ruth, virtually impells her, against Margaret's judgment, to become the new mistress of Howards End.

For all their differences, the Schlegels and Wilcoxes are rich. Leonard Bast, the novel's other key character, is poor. A young clerk, who lives in a squalid London flat with his mistress – later his wife – Jacky, he tries to relieve the tedium of existence by going to concerts and reading Ruskin and other 'improving' writers. 'One guessed him,' writes Forster, 'as the third generation, grandson to the shepherd or ploughboy whom civilization had sucked into the town; as one of the thousands who have lost the life of the body and failed to reach the life of the spirit.' (A113; K132) Victimized by the outer life, Leonard cannot give more than sporadic attention to the inner. Spiritually he is in no-man's-land, a fragmented being who will never be whole.

If Forster were Charles Dickens, Leonard would doubtless be a convincing character and *Howards End* a more satisfactory novel. But like Henry Wilcox, Leonard is one of the novel's failures, for Forster had no firsthand knowledge of what it feels like to be poor and ambitious. He does not, for he cannot, give one the sense of a direct encounter with Leonard's mind, but instead comments ironically upon its workings, as in the well-known scene in which Leonard is reading Ruskin. There, looking over the young man's shoulder, he mockingly adapts one of Ruskin's sentences to a description of Leonard's flat: 'Let us consider a little each of these characters in succession, and first (for of the absence of ventilation enough has been said already), what is very peculiar to this flat – its obscurity.' Then, encouraged by the effect of the parody, he ridicules Ruskin:

And the voice in the gondola rolled on, piping melodiously of Effort and Self-Sacrifice, full of high purpose, full of beauty, full even of sympathy and the love of men, yet somehow eluding all that was actual and insistent in Leonard's life. For it was the voice of one who had never been dirty or hungry, and had not guessed successfully what dirt and hunger are. (A47)

Had Forster, one wonders, a more intimate contact with dirt and hunger? Finally, with compassionate irony, he shifts the emphasis to Leonard:

Leonard listened to it with reverence. He felt that he was being done good to, and that if he kept on with Ruskin, and the Queen's Hall Concerts, and some pictures by Watts, he would one day push his head out of the grey waters and see the universe. He believed in sudden conversion, a belief which may be right, but which is peculiarly attractive to a half-baked mind. (A47; K58–9)

Such commentary, of course, tells us less about Leonard than about his creator as he considers, from his comfortable vantage, the hopelessness of his character's plight.

The plot of *Howards End* is contrived to effect a partial synthesis of its antithetical elements. Margaret is to marry Henry, Helen to have a child by Leonard; then, in the final chapter, Margaret and Henry, with Helen and the child, will settle at Howards End, of which Margaret becomes the acknowledged mistress.

Like Forster's earlier novels and *A Passage to India*, *Howards End* can be read as a *Bildungsreise*. Helen and Margaret, the principal travellers, must venture forth from their comfortable surroundings to explore new kinds of experience in an uncertain and sometimes dangerous world, and from their journey, to become spiritually enriched. The fact that they do not travel to foreign lands (except for Helen's two trips to Germany, where the reader is not permitted to follow her) should not blind one to the nature and importance of their travels. Going from Wickham Place into less sheltered parts of London and into the country, they become precariously involved with the Wilcoxes and the Basts, people whose outlooks are radically different from theirs, and from whom theirs will be enlarged.

Forster underscores the travel theme and helps to offset the insularity of the novel's setting by his many references to seas, rivers, and tides. Connecting the known with the unknown, the sea symbolizes the universe, formless, illimitable, and challenging, in which man must try to chart a course. Wickham Place, where the Schlegels live, is a 'backwater' or 'estuary' that will be 'swept away in time' (A5; K11). We learn of London's 'grey tides' (A106; K124) threatening to sweep the Londoner 'away from his moorings' (A107; K125) and of its 'shallows' washing against the surrounding countryside (A106; K124). Its thoroughfares are likened to tides (A42; K53) and it is said to be in a 'continual flux' (A106; K124). Within this great sea, the Schlegels stand 'upon money as upon islands', their feet 'above the waves', while those less fortunate lie 'below the surface' (A58; K71). From their backwater, Margaret and Helen look enviously out at the Wilcoxes, whose 'hands [are] on all the ropes' (A25; K34), while Margaret, feeling the 'vessel of life...slipping past her' (A147; K173), would like to join forces with them. But the Wilcoxes' voyage is without romance, for romance requires a sense of adventure and a desire for the unknown, and the Wilcoxes – Ruth excepted – have no taste for either. Travelling chiefly for business, they sedulously try to avoid the dangerous 'rocks of emotion', just as Ulysses' sailors 'voyaged past the Sirens, having first stopped one another's ears with wool' (A99; K117). Before boarding the vessel of life, Margaret is simply 'a curious seeker' standing at 'the verge of the sea that tells so little but tells a little', and the impact on her of Ruth Wilcox is likened to that of a 'great wave' that strews at her feet 'fragments torn from the unknown' (A100; K118). Helen, as already noted, after the debacle at Oniton, is said to have the look of a shipwrecked sailor. At the end of the novel, Margaret hears the Wilcoxes bidding each other goodbye, and their words strike her as 'like the ebb of a dying sea' (A340; K392). It is the sea upon which she and Helen have sailed and by which they have come to the green world of Howards End.

References to rivers and tides underscore the novelist's vision of an ever-changing world through which the traveller must pass. For example, the rivers and tides so conspicuous *River and tides* in Forster's panoramic description of England in chapter 19 contribute to the sense of a richly varied, dynamic country whose ultimate destiny no one can foresee:

There was a long silence, during which the tide returned into Poole Harbour. ..The water crept over the mud-flats towards the gorse and the blackened heather. Branksea Island lost its immense foreshores, and became a sombre episode of trees. Frome was forced inward towards Dorchester, Stour against Wimborne, Avon towards Salisbury, and over the immense displacement the sun presided, leading it to triumph ere he sank to rest. England was alive, throbbing through all her estuaries, crying for joy through the mouths of all her gulls, and the north wind, with contrary motion, blew stronger against her rising seas. What did it mean? For what end are her fair complexities, her changes of soil, her sinuous coast? Does she belong to those who have moulded her and made her feared by other lands, or to those who have added nothing to her power, but have somehow seen her, seen the whole island at once, lying as a jewel in a silver sea, sailing as a ship of souls, with all the brave world's fleet accompanying her towards eternity? (A172; K200–1)

In an earlier scene in which Margaret and Helen run into Henry on the Chelsea Embankment, Forster uses their differing response to the Thames as a way of revealing their antithetical attitudes to modern life. To Margaret and Helen, the river is sad and mysterious, Margaret seeing in its shifting tides and everlasting flow a suggestion of the flux and formlessness of life. The sight of the ebbing tide reminds her of modern man's inability to take root:

The tide had begun to ebb. Margaret leant over the parapet and watched it sadly. Mr Wilcox had forgotten his wife, Helen her lover; she herself was probably forgetting. Every one moving. Is it worth while attempting the past when there is this continual flux even in the hearts of men? (A134; K157)

Later, alone with Henry, she exclaims, 'I hate this continual flux of London...I mistrust rivers, even in scenery.' (A179; K209) Henry, however, sees the Thames as a symbol of progress. 'Shows things are moving. Good for trade.' (A179; K209) And he glances down at the full tide 'cheerfully' (A133; K155).

Margaret and Helen, then, are the novel's key travellers in a shifting world of hidden depths and other dangers in which self-fulfilment and defeat are equally possible. Both women are endowed with a sense of adventure, a desire for what Forster calls the unseen, and both see their voyage as a means to spiritual reward.

Margaret, not Helen, is the heroine, because it is only Margaret who, when the three connected crises of the novel occur – the disclosure of Henry's adultery, of Helen's pregnancy, and of Leonard's death – demonstrates the love, compassion, and the sense of proportion needed to establish harmony. Disdaining 'the heroic equipment' (A247; K286), she nevertheless performs heroically. On the verge of abandoning Henry and going with Helen to Germany following Leonard's death, she finally remains with him, an exhausted and broken man, and reconciles him and Helen to one another. 'You did it all,' exclaims Helen, '...you picked up the pieces, and made us a home. Can't it strike you – even for a moment – that your life has been heroic?' (A336; K388)

Helen, on the other hand, tries to be heroic and fails. Taking up Leonard's cause in the name of Truth and Justice by melodramatically bringing him and Jacky to Evie Wilcox's wedding-party, she inadvertently paves the way for Leonard's death. Her action recalls Harriet Herriton's even brasher attempt to secure 'justice' for Gino's baby by kidnapping the child, in *Where Angels Fear to Tread*. Such extremism, both novels suggest, can be disastrous. Forster, who claims to distrust Great Men and the radical social surgery they frequently advocate,[6] puts more faith in the less spectacular, mediating force of people like Margaret.

Margaret, then, is a heroine in spite of herself. Yet her final triumph is facilitated by a chain of events over which she has little, if any, control. To Helen's assertion that her sister has been heroic, Margaret replies, without false modesty, 'No doubt I have done a little towards straightening the tangle, but things that I can't phrase have helped me.' (A337; K388)

What Margaret can't phrase is the fact that almost every incident and character in the novel have contributed to her success. Like Lucy Honeychurch, she has been caught in a circumstantial web, and if matters have turned out well for some, badly for others, much has depended on luck, or, to put it another way, on the manipulating hand of the novelist.

No novel of Forster's is more obviously contrived, for in no other novel has he had to strain credibility and coincidence so much in order to bring his antitheses together. Wilcoxes, Schlegels, and Basts are three groups of characters socially and psychologically so far apart that in the normal course of events there is no reason why they should become intimately involved with one another. Furthermore, the fact that their involvement must be sustained over a considerable period (the novel's time-span is approximately four years) if the desired results are to be plausibly achieved aggravates the need for contrivance.

That the Schlegels meet the Wilcoxes and Leonard in the first place is, of course, the result of chance. The spring before the novel's action begins, they happened to meet Henry and Ruth in Germany on a holiday. At the Queen's Hall concert, they find themselves next to Leonard, and when Helen accidentally walks home with the young man's umbrella, she paves the way for their further acquaintance. After Helen's visit to Howards End and her broken engagement to Paul, there is

---

[6] *Two Cheers for Democracy*, 73. Harcourt, Brace, New York, 1951.

no compelling reason for the Wilcoxes and Schlegels to see each other again. Forster, however, assures their continued relationship by temporarily moving the Wilcoxes not simply to London, but next door to Wickham Place. The move permits Ruth and Margaret to become friends and Ruth to decide to will her Howards End. Having so decided, Ruth speedily dies.

Two years elapse during which the Schlegels and Wilcoxes see little of one another; and indeed the latter, having destroyed Ruth's eccentric will, would have every reason, one would assume, for wanting to break off relations. But Forster, of course, cannot allow this, and brings them together by the simple device of having Helen and Margaret run in to Henry on the Chelsea Embankment.

In the meantime, Leonard, who, following the umbrella episode, had seen no more of the Schlegels, has been returned to the scene of action by means of a more elaborate device: Jacky's discovery of the visiting-card that Margaret had given Leonard two years before. First Jacky arrives at Wickham Place, ostensibly seeking her husband, who had not been home for a couple of nights; then, the next day, Leonard calls with an explanation: he had gone for a long nocturnal walk in the Surrey hills. Margaret and Helen are impressed. Non-U though he is, Leonard is obviously a romantic, and deserves help. And it is of how to help Leonard that they are talking when they run in to Henry on the Embankment.

The way is thus clear for Henry to involve himself with Leonard's life. Obviously, he tells the girls, the young man should give up his job with the Porphyrion Life Insurance Company, which, according to Henry, will soon be bankrupt. Margaret and Helen relay this piece of advice to Leonard, who, acting upon it, contributes to his destruction.

The chance meeting on the Embrankment also paves the way for Margaret's marriage to Henry, the most damagingly contrived of the novel's features. Henry, as noted, possesses not a single attribute that a woman like Margaret could conceivably love. In fact, she sees right through to his spiritual hollowness. She and Henry, moreover, both seem to consider sex a nasty business, and Margaret yearns for a pallid substitute that she calls comradeship (A183, 203, 237; K213, 236, 274 & *passim*). Nevertheless, despite their comparatively sexless relationship, Margaret is actuated by a wish to unify her own and Henry's fragmented lives and to help Henry build 'the rainbow bridge that should connect the prose in us with the passion' (A183; K213); but what kind of passion is compatible with comradeship is unclear.

rainbow bridge

To bring his major antitheses – Wilcoxes, Schlegels, and Basts – into climactic juxtaposition, Forster contrives the most melodramatic of the novel's scenes: that of Evie Wilcox's wedding-party, with the arrival of Helen, Leonard, and Jacky, and the farfetched disclosure that Jacky is none other than Henry Wilcox's former mistress. That Margaret's marriage survives the resulting strain is as much due to circumstances over which she has no control as to her own fortitude.

Three of the novel's minor characters – Aunt Juley, Miss Avery, and Tibby – help to bring matters to a head. By becoming critically ill just when Helen is needed to shock Henry and everyone else with her pregnancy, Aunt Juley serves to recall her from Germany, to which she had fled after her night with Leonard. In the meantime, Miss Avery, the old caretaker of Howards End, sets the stage for the novel's climax, and thereby becomes the indirect agent of Leonard's death and of a new life for Margaret and Helen. The Schlegels' furniture and other belongings having been stored at Howards End because of the expiration of their lease. Miss Avery arranges it in the various rooms, putting the books and the family sword in the downstairs hall. When Leonard arrives on the fatal morning to confess to Margaret his 'seduction' of Helen, Charles Wilcox seizes the sword and begins to thrash him with it; whereupon Leonard, to save himself, grabs onto the bookcase full of books, pulls it on top of himself, and is immediately killed.[7] Even the passive and self-indulgent Tibby is

---

[7] The fact and manner of Leonard's death are, of course, fortuitous. A note in Forster's hand in the MS at King's College shows that he considered three

implicated in Leonard's death. Succumbing to Charles's bully-
ing interrogation, he inadvertently betrays to him the name
of Helen's 'seducer'. Thus, though a would-be neutral who
would prefer to sit on the sidelines and cultivate his mind,
Tibby becomes an inextricable part of the novel's network.
The merest coincidence also contributes to Leonard's death.
Catching a glimpse of Margaret and Tibby in St Paul's,
Leonard suddenly conceives the idea of going to her to confess, which brings him to Howards End. Hence Margaret's
eventual happiness, which involves death and destruction,
depends only in part upon her own character. Like a heroine
in a Greek tragedy, she is controlled as well as controlling.

In the final chapter, the antitheses achieve a qualified and
precarious resolution. Margaret, we are told, has triumphed.
'She, who had never expected to conquer any one, had
charged straight through these Wilcoxes and broken up their
lives.' (A339; K391) She and Henry, with Helen and her baby,
are peacefully settled at Howards End, of which Margaret is
mistress. Outside the harvest is being reaped.

And yet the brown haze of London on the horizon warns
that Howards End cannot endure indefinitely. The world is
becoming increasingly urbanized, and what Forster regards as
the country's superior values cannot hold out forever.

Margaret's 'triumph', moreover, is a curiously limited one.
She had wanted to unite her feminine inner life with a mascu-
line representative of the outer one, and had hoped to enrich
Henry's life by connecting 'the prose in him with the passion'.
Ambitious aims, and largely unrealized. Henry has simply
been transformed from a strong shell of a man to a weak one.
The grit she had once admired in him is gone, and she will
build for him, one feels, no 'rainbow bridge'. Unlike the first
Mrs Wilcox, who lived in harmony with her entire family,
Margaret appears to have incurred her step-children's per-
manent enmity. Her marriage, furthermore, will be childless.

other possibilities: (1) that Leonard kill Charles and then fling himself out
of the window; (2) that Leonard and Helen both die; (3) that Leonard
remain alive.

'I do not love children,' she tells Helen. 'I am thankful to have none. I can play with their beauty and charm, but that is all – nothing real, not one scrap of what there ought to be.' (A335; K387) The lives of both sisters are still incomplete: Helen has *ending* a child but no husband; Margaret, a husband but no child. Finally, Margaret's settlement at Howards End constitutes a visible retreat from the world she had once professed to admire, not a stronger connection with it. Like some of the characters in Forster's early short stories, she has escaped to an 'other kingdom'.

The novel's highly qualified resolution reflects, I feel, the tentative nature of Forster's belief in the power of liberalism, or any other 'ism', to heal the fragmentations of modern life. Life, he declares, is essentially chaotic (A105; K123); consequently, the most one can accomplish is to create within this chaos islands of order. These islands, however, like Wickham Place, will give way in time, and new ones must be created. Perhaps one of the reasons that Forster wrote *Howards End* was to discover whether individuals in the modern world might indeed contribute to an enduring order; but the only enduring reality, the novel suggests, is chaos, of which the city is a reflection.

Howards End has many weaknesses. Besides the poorly conceived characters already mentioned and a sometimes crudely managed plot, there is a good deal of coy or sentimental authorial comment, much of which attempts to control the reader's response to characters. Margaret's view, for example, that the portals of King's Cross Station suggest infinity is undercut with a facetious apology: 'If you think this ridiculous, remember that it is not Margaret who is telling you about it.' (A9, K16) Suspecting that Leonard's account of his nocturnal walk may not impress the reader, Forster tries to fortify it with a comment so ill-judged as to guarantee the reverse. 'You may laugh at him, you who have slept nights out on the veldt, with your rifle beside you and all the atmosphere of adventure pat. And you also may laugh who think adventures silly. But do not be surprised if Leonard is shy whenever he meets you, and if the Schlegels rather than Jacky hear about the dawn.' (A122; K142) To be told, as a clincher, that Leonard has 'the heart of a man ticking fast in his chest' (A122; K143) seems unlikely to win the reader's sympathy. Mrs Wilcox, a thin character, is also inflated by Forster's comments. She 'possesses the instinctive wisdom that the past can alone bestow' (A19; K28) and gives 'the idea of greatness' (A73; K89). These and other such remarks indicate not merely a failure of technique; they are symptomatic of Forster's inability to control his vision. They suggest that he is trying to force both himself and the reader to take seriously characters and values that he inwardly sees as ineffective or false.

These and other faults notwithstanding, *Howards End* is a richly suggestive novel. It is larger than its immediate subject, the involvement of a couple of Edwardian ladies with a businessman and his family and with a struggling young clerk. It deals perceptively with timeless human relationships and with a defining characteristic of modern life, the divorce between man's inner and outer worlds. Its best scenes, such as the Queen's Hall concert, Aunt Juley's journey to Howards End, and Margaret's shopping expedition with Mrs Wilcox, blend wit and humour with compassion and insight.

One probable reason for the novel's popularity is that, for all its pessimistic insight into certain aspects of modern life, it has a romantic and optimistic side. Life, it suggests, may be chaotic and dangerous, yet for the brave and sensitive, it offers a chance for adventure and love. Depressed by his work, his flat, and his mistress, Leonard can escape to Queen's Hall and walk under the stars in the Surrey Hills. More fortunate than he, his son may also 'take the great chances of beauty and adventure that the world offers' (A327; K379). Life is a voyage into the unknown, and those with whom Forster generally sympathizes have the courage to take the risks that the unknown demands. When Aunt Juley, upon learning that the Wilcoxes are moving next door to Wickham Place, warns Margaret and Helen to be 'careful', Margaret demurs. 'Those who prepare for all the emergencies of life beforehand,' she

feels, 'may equip themselves at the expense of joy.' (A57; K70)
'The most successful career,' writes Forster,

must show a waste of strength that might have removed mountains, and the
most unsuccessful is not that of the man who is taken unprepared, but of him
who has prepared and is never taken. On a tragedy of that kind our national
morality is duly silent. It assumes that preparation against danger is in itself
a good, and that men, like nations, are the better for staggering through life
fully armed. (A104; K123)

Plunging unprepared into the great sea of life, Margaret and
Helen are matured and humanized.

The world, moreover, is not entirely chaotic. Here and there
is order and a degree of stability. Contrasting with the seas,
rivers, and tides, so prominent in the novel's imagery, is the
landscape of Howards End, fixed and harmonious, symbolizing a life rooted for centuries in the soil. 'In these English
farms, if anywhere,' muses Margaret, 'one might see life
steadily and see it whole, group in one vision its transitoriness
and its eternal youth, connect – connect without bitterness
until all men are brothers.' (A266; K308) That is the novel's
ultimate vision: the brotherhood of man as a goal to strive for,
though never, perhaps, to be achieved.

6

Maurice

I

Maurice is the narrowest and least resonant of Forster's six novels. Forster views Maurice and his world solely in relation to Maurice's homosexuality; and Maurice himself is so obsessed with his problem that he relates everything else to it. His obsession, of course, is understandable: he lives not in a world in which 'Gay is Beautiful', but in England before the First World War, a country that only a few years before the time of the novel had sent Oscar Wilde to prison for sodomy. In its preoccupation with the protagonist's sexuality, *Maurice* markedly contrasts with *Howards End* and *A Passage to India*. Obviously, between the composition of his two most wide-ranging novels, Forster felt a special need to give fictional perspective to a problem of the deepest personal concern.

Maurice's life, like that of other Forsterian travellers, is a psychological journey, leading in Maurice's case from inner darkness to inner light.[1] Sojourning in various places, each with its special values and opportunities, Maurice is led to realize his sexuality and then to try to accommodate it to the demands of society. Only after prolonged struggle and doubt does he find in his love for a man of totally different class and background the means to salvation.

The first phase of his journey, his boyhood and adolescence, serves to awaken his sexuality, and to encourage him to repress it – to live, that is, a lie; an unhappy condition for which his home and school, and lack of self-confidence are all partly responsible. When the novel opens, Maurice Hall is fourteen. Like Rickie Elliot, whom psychologically he somewhat resembles, he grows up in a comfortable suburban house, over which

---

[1] Imagery of light and dark recurs throughout the novel to suggest the social and psychological forces afflicting Maurice.

his widowed and doting mother presides. On her only son, she lavishes a sticky solicitude, which he willingly accepts. His two younger sisters, Ada and Kitty, also cater to him.

Two incidents during his early adolescence help to undermine his confidence in adult authority and contribute to his sexual bent. The first, which opens the novel, is the sex lecture that Mr Ducie, one of his preparatory-school teachers, gives him as they walk along the beach together during a school outing. With the aid of diagrams traced in the sand, Mr Ducie presents the 'facts', which Maurice dutifully attends to, though they bear no apparent relation to his own feelings. The lecture over, master and boy walk on; but when some strangers approach the spot where they had been, Mr Ducie, realizing that he has forgotten to erase the diagrams, runs back in a panic to do so. He need not have bothered, for the rising tide has done it for him. The lecture, coupled with Mr Ducie's panic, fills Maurice with a profound mistrust. '"Liar," he thought. "Liar, coward, he's told me nothing."' (9)[2]

His sense of betrayal is heightened when, upon going home, he finds that his one real friend, George, the garden-boy, has suddenly left the family employ. Was he discharged, as his mother declares, because he was getting too old? Or did he, as Mr Howell, the coachman, tells Maurice, leave of his own accord? The question is never resolved. George's departure leaves Maurice feeling sad and friendless, and eventually gives rise to two semi-erotic dreams about the boy, both of which clearly point the way in which Maurice is going. Like Lucy Honeychurch after she was caught kissing another George, he is now thoroughly muddled, his inability to confront his own needs being suggested by his difficulty in adjusting to light and dark when he goes to bed at night.

The trouble was the looking-glass. He did not mind seeing his face in it, nor casting a shadow on the ceiling reflected in the glass. He would arrange the candle so as to avoid the combination, and then dare himself to put it back and be gripped with fear. He knew what it was, it reminded him of nothing horrible. But he was afraid. In the end he would dash out the candle and

---

[2] All references to pages in Maurice are to the Arnold, 1971 edition.

leap into bed. Total darkness he could bear, but this room had the further defect of being opposite a street lamp. On good nights the light would penetrate the curtains unalarmingly, but sometimes blots like skulls fell over the furniture. His heart beat violently, and he lay in terror, with all his household close at hand.

Sunnington, Maurice's public school, ends the first stage of his journey. Having barely survived a recent sex scandal, the school firmly discourages any open interest in sex among the boys, with the result that Maurice, longing for smut, hears little, and his 'chief indecencies' are solitary. He has now descended into the 'Valley of the Shadow of Life' (14).

Cambridge provides the means by which he will leave the 'Valley'. Here for the first time he finds himself – as Rickie Elliot did before him – in an atmosphere that encourages him to be himself.

People turned out to be alive. Hitherto he had supposed that they *were* what he *pretended* to be – flat pieces of cardboard stamped with a conventional design – but as he strolled about the courts at night and saw through the windows some men singing and others arguing and others at their books, there came by no process of reason a conviction that they were human beings with feelings akin to his own. (22)

All that is needed now is a friend to help Maurice realize the hidden truth about himself; and this friend he finds in Clive Durham.

It is an attraction of opposites, Clive standing in roughly the same psychological relation to Maurice as Stewart Ansell stood to Rickie. A year older than Maurice, Clive is more cultivated and more refined. Having long known himself to be homosexual, he has renounced Christianity, his family's religion, in favour of a fashionable Platonism, Plato appearing not merely to countenance, but actually to extol, love between men. Until he meets Maurice, Clive has expressed his homosexuality only in 'tender emotions' for other undergraduates; but he is willing to 'go further should he consider it right' (62).

Forster traces their growing friendship with considerable insight. Like Stewart and Rickie, the two men begin with horseplay and the exchange of confidences about their families. Intellectually the more sophisticated, Clive then undermines Maurice's uncritical Christian orthodoxy and suggests that he read Plato's *Symposium*. Maurice, however, cannot relate Plato to himself, any more than he could Mr Ducie's sex lecture; and when Clive, counting on Plato to have shown Maurice the light, tells Maurice that he loves him, the latter is 'shocked to the bottom of his suburban soul' and turns away in disgust.

The inident, however, is the catalyst that unites them. Maurice's nature is merely 'slow'. Realizing that he, too, loves Clive and that he has run the risk of losing him for good, he climbs one night through Clive's bedroom window and tells him he loves him.

The result for both men is happiness, short-lived though it is. One day they cut lectures and ride on Maurice's motor cycle into the country – an 'eternal moment' never to be repeated. For cutting classes and being rude to the Dean, Maurice is 'sent down' and compelled to begin his career as a stockbroker.

From this point on, his friendship with Clive runs into obstacles. In the protective atmosphere of Cambridge it had flowered; now, confronted with the more hostile verities of the outside world, it begins to founder. Maurice's job in the city is one check; Clive's family responsibility, another. As the only male, he must take time to manage Penge, the Durham's deteriorating estate on the Wilts–Somerset border, and become active in local politics. His mother, moreover, expects him to marry and provide Penge with an heir.

Despite difficulties, Clive and Maurice continue to see each other and remain as happy 'as men under that star can expect' (89). Matters might have continued so until, perhaps tiring of the affair, they drifted apart. But Forster's plan will not allow this to happen. Maurice's love for Clive is merely a prelude; it has awakened him to his sexual nature and enlarged his capacity to love; but it has been too easy. Before Maurice can be saved, he must be tested. Without Clive's support, he must pit his homosexual needs against the heterosexual demands of society. He must experience a crisis.

The crisis comes when Clive suddenly turns heterosexual;

a change that must startle the reader almost as much as it startles Maurice, for nothing in Clive's character has prepared us to expect it. Remarking that 'the body is deeper than the soul and its secrets inscrutable', Forster simply imposes the change on him as a way of bringing about the crisis. Clive's 'conversion' is significantly associated with illness – with flu and diarrhea, through which Maurice, his sister Ada, and a trained nurse all care for him. But it is the women who impress Clive. Recovering, he goes alone to Greece; and there, sitting in the empty theatre of Dionysus and seeing only 'a dying light and a dead land', he realizes that he is 'normal'.

With the loss of Clive, Maurice enters the *Sturm und Drang* stage of his journey. By various shifts he tries to overcome his sense of loss and sublimate his sex drive; joining the Territorials, supporting social work, subscribing to charities, playing football with the youths of a college settlement and teaching them boxing and arithmetic. But when Dickie Barry, the schoolboy nephew of the Halls' family doctor, stays at the Halls', Maurice comes perilously close to trying to seduce him.

Horrified by his lust, Maurice decides to consult a doctor. If he cannot sublimate sex, perhaps he can normalize it; for one of the ironies of his situation is that he would like to have children. He goes, accordingly, to see Dr Barry, an aging, cynical one-time lady-killer, and, to the reader, obviously the worst kind of person to ask for advice of this nature. Dismissing the problem as 'rubbish, rubbish', Barry tells him to put on his clothes and have a whisky.

On the recommendation of a homosexual college friend, Risley, Maurice then visits a hypnotist of questionable credentials, Dr Lasker Jones, a bloodless 'scientific' type, who dispassionately diagnoses Maurice's problem as 'congenital homosexuality' and proceeds through hypnotism to try to awaken him to the pleasures of women. But Maurice is not so easily to be changed. Though he succumbs to the doctor's hypnotic influence and sees a picture on the pictureless office wall, the picture he sees is not, as the doctor insists, that of a woman, but of a man.[3] While hypnotized, Maurice also re-dreams the second of the two semi-erotic dreams provoked by the departure of George, the garden-boy – a dream of a voice saying, 'This is your friend.' Disappointed in the results of his visit, but not despairing, Maurice arranges to see the doctor again.

In the meantime, he has met at Penge – though he has yet to recognize him as such – the 'friend' who is to prove his salvation: Alec Scudder, Clive Durham's assistant game-keeper. Scudder, it should be said at the outset, is probably the novel's greatest flaw – an utterly unconvincing character. He has characteristics aplenty, most of them unattractive – ambition, aggressiveness, slyness, pride, and solicitude among them; but they do not merge into a believable human being. Consequently, the love between him and Maurice is equally unconvincing. Most of Scudder's speech consists of clipped wooden phrases, of which the following, addressed to Maurice when the two are in bed together, is a depressing and fairly characteristic sample: 'Nice you and me like this...who'd have thought...First time I ever seed you I thought, "Wish I and that one..." just like that... "wouldn't I and him..." and it is so.' (214) Not surprisingly, Forster gives us only shallow interior glimpses of the man, for he had little insight into the minds of the lower classes.

Scudder's salvatory role depends not simply upon his and Maurice's love for each other, but on what Scudder is and represents. As the gamekeeper, he is associated with the only vital feature of Clive's estate, the plant and animal life. Like Howard Sholten in 'The Purple Envelope', he likes to hunt; the gun that he carries when he mounts the ladder into Maurice's bedroom symbolizing his potentially destructive vitality. Scudder has one other attribute necessary to Maurice's salvation: he is not a 'gentleman', a fact that, coupled with his supposed vitality, will enable Maurice to escape the restraints of his own class.

[3] In the 1913 typescript version of the novel in King's College Library, Cambridge, Maurice's response to the picture is more ambivalent. It changes 'now at his will, now against it, from male to female'.

But the means of escape are not to be easy. Following Scudder's remarkable climb, gun in hand, through Maurice's window and their ensuing night together, it is beset with difficulties. First there is the problem of Maurice himself. As Forster emphasizes in his 'Terminal Note' to the novel, his protagonist is 'rather a snob'. He regards servants as his natural inferiors, and after his night with Scudder at Penge, is overwhelmed with guilt and anxiety. Not only, he feels, has he violated his host's trust and the code of their class, but he has paved the way for a possible scandal. A further encounter with Scudder could, consequently, be dangerous. A telegram from Scudder asking to spend the night with him in the Boat House at Penge, which Maurice receives when he returns home, does nothing to allay his anxiety. How has the game-keeper got his address? And what might the local post-office, which handled the telegram, think? Maurice decides to ignore Scudder's request, considering it a species of blackmail and a punishment for having gone 'outside his class'. His second visit to Lasker Jones is a failure, for he is now torn between a sense of 'noblesse oblige' and a craving for Scudder.

The latter, too, as Maurice will soon learn, is limited by his class and outlook. Far from being a simple 'son of the woods', he is resentful of being treated like the servant he is, and keen to get ahead in the world. Consequently, when Maurice ignores his appeal, Scudder's pride and resentment goad him into sending Maurice an overtly threatening letter. '. . . I don't think it fair to treat me like a dog... *I know about you and Mr Durham*...I am not your servant, I will not be treated as your servant...' (201) By now, however, Maurice, feeling half-ready to throw over his profession and take to the 'greenwood' with Alec, can take a fairly charitable view of the letter, and he agrees to meet its author the next day in the British Museum.

To bring matters to a head, Forster has introduced a re-maining complication: Alec is to leave the following week with his brother Fred for the Argentine, where he hopes to make his fortune. But for this circumstance, Maurice might have taken drastic action to end the affair, either by putting himself in the hands of a solicitor or possibly by committing suicide. But the imminence of Scudder's departure, besides sharpening Maurice's craving for him, appears to diminish the need for any such drastic action.

Their meeting in the British Museum and ensuing night together provide the turning-point. In the Museum, Maurice is calm and agreeable, and his refusal to be intimidated by Scudder's threats, even when Mr Ducie, Maurice's old teacher, unexpectedly turns up and almost recognizes his former pupil, wins Scudder's heart and admiration. Scudder is still, however, determined, as he tells Maurice, to sail in three days for the Argentine.

The resolution comes quickly. When, against his better judgment, Maurice goes down to the boat to see Scudder off and Scudder fails to show up, Maurice knows intuitively that his lover has changed his mind and will take to the greenwood with him. He finds him, as he expects, in the Boat House at Penge.

All that remains to be done, Maurice feels, before they take off together, is to close the final chapter on his association with Clive. The one-time Platonist, now a prosaically married country squire, who had raised Maurice out of the 'Valley of the Shadow of Life' and helped to make him the 'outlaw' he is about to become, is in his study preparing an election campaign. When Maurice tells him that he loves the gamekeeper, it is Clive's turn to be shocked, just as Maurice had once been shocked when Clive had confessed his love for him. Maurice's confession appropriately takes place outside in the dark, among the flowers and shrubs where he had once collided with Scudder. Like that which had frightened him when he went to bed as a boy, the darkness is not merely physical: it is the psychological darkness in which he has dwelt and from which, as the falling petals of the evening primroses suggest, he is about to emerge. Having confessed, he vanishes forever from Clive's life, leaving him – and the reader – to speculate on his future.[4]

[4] In the 1913 version, Forster added a bucolic epilogue in which Maurice's sister Kitty, still unmarried and now twenty-seven, bicycling through the

II

For all its sensitivity and perceptiveness, *Maurice* is the most patently flawed of Forster's novels. For one thing, its construction is weak. In an attempt, presumably, to broaden the novel's range, Forster dwells too much on some of the minor characters – for example, Maurice's sisters, Clive's sister and her fiancé Archie London, and the shadowy guests at Penge – none of whom are interesting in their own right. But the character who does most to throw the novel off balance is Clive Durham. In the Cambridge section, Forster devotes so much attention to Clive and his background that, reading *Maurice* for the first time, one might easily assume that the novel was to be centrally concerned with not one, but two, homosexuals of contrasting temperament. Clive's primary role, of course, is catalystic. He is mainly introduced to contribute to Maurice's sexual development and the crisis he undergoes, and to enable him to meet Alec Scudder. Having led Maurice to realize that he is homosexual, Clive has fulfilled his major purpose; and Forster, as he admits in his 'Terminal Note', loses interest in him, killing him off in spirit, though not in flesh. Had he accomplished the latter as well, it would have been better for the novel, since he would not then have felt obliged to detail Clive's post-Cambridge existence – detail largely irrelevant to Forster's principal subject and concerning a character who, after his conversion to normalcy, holds no more interest for the reader than he holds for the novelist.

Forster's uncertain control is also evident in his conception of Maurice and in his attitude towards him. He cannot really decide what kind of man his protagonist is. 'In Maurice,' he writes, 'I tried to create a character who was completely unlike

woods on a holiday, meets Alec and Maurice, a couple of itinerant wood-cutters. Though Maurice's clothes are ragged, he is in good shape. '...a new man throbbed – tougher, more centralised...' Later, speculating on her brother's life, Kitty concludes that 'he must be very fond of his mate, he must have given up us on his account, I should imagine they are practically in love'. Afraid, however, that Kitty may tell the police about them, Maurice and Alec decide to move to another neighbourhood. Forster concludes that at least they were 'together for the moment, they too had stayed disintegration and combined daily work with love; and who can hope for more?'.

myself or what I supposed myself to be: someone handsome, healthy, bodily attractive, mentally torpid, not a bad business man and rather a snob.' (236) Forster's wish to make Maurice as unlike himself as possible must have been partly impelled by a felt need to distance himself from his protagonist's problem if he was to write a successful novel about it. But the fact is that Maurice bears a family likeness to the protagonists in Forster's first three novels; especially, as noted, to Rickie and Lucy, who, together with Philip, are partly self-portraits. Like all three protagonists, he is sensitive and lacking self-confidence; consequently, easily muddled.

That he strongly resembles these characters is not in itself a fault. The fault largely results from Forster's uncertain relationship to his hero. Forster often views Maurice with sympathetic, yet ironic, detachment, as when, for instance, he remarks that Maurice was 'a mediocre member of a mediocre school, and left a faint and favourable impression behind.' (14) Too often, however, he identifies himself with his hero. In the following passage, for example, which occurs soon after Maurice decides to meet Scudder in the British Museum, Maurice and his creator are clearly one in their assessment of Maurice's business partners:

His new vigour persisted next morning, when he returned to work. Before his failure with Lasker Jones he had looked forward to work as a privilege of which he was almost unworthy. It was to have rehabilitated him, so that he could hold up his head at home. But now it too crumbled, and again he wanted to laugh, and wondered why he had been taken in so long. The clientele of Messrs Hill and Hall was drawn from the middle-middle classes, whose highest desire seemed shelter – continuous shelter – not a lair in the darkness to be reached against fear, but shelter everywhere and always, until the existence of earth and sky is forgotten, shelter from poverty and disease and violence and impoliteness; and consequently from joy; God slipped this retribution in. He saw from their faces, as from the faces of his clerks and his partners, that they had never known real joy. Society had catered for them too completely. They had never struggled, and only a struggle twists sentimentality and lust together into love. Maurice would have been a good lover. He could have given and taken serious pleasure. But in these men the strands were untwisted; they were either fatuous or obscene, and in his present mood he despised the latter least. They would come to him and ask for a safe six per cent security. He would reply, 'You can't combine high interest with safety – it isn't to be done;' and in the end they would say, 'How would it be if I invested most of my money at four per cent, and play about with an odd hundred?' Even so did they speculate in a little vice – not in too much, lest it disorganized domesticity, but in enough to show that their virtue was sham. And until yesterday he had cringed to them.

Only two sentences – 'Maurice would have been a good lover. He could have given and taken serious pleasure' – are clearly Forster's comment alone. If Maurice were consistently presented as an acute and articulate social critic, such a passage could be defended. In *Emma*, for example, Jane Austen and her heroine sometimes view another character through the same eyes, for both women possess a similarly ironic cast of mind. But Maurice, Forster tells us, is 'mentally torpid', his brain is 'his weakest organ' (31). Is it likely, then, even under his present stress, that he would be capable of such insights as the foregoing passage conveys?

The same criticism applies to the following passage in which Maurice, having gone down to the boat to see Scudder off for South America, runs into the Reverend Borenius, the minister at Penge, and realizes that the latter is suddenly suspicious of Maurice's presence on the boat:

He was certain that the rector had guessed, or rather that a wave of recognition had passed. A man of the world would have suspected nothing – Mr Ducie hadn't – but this man had a special sense, being spiritual, and could scent out invisible emotions. Ascetisism and piety had their practical side. They can generate insight, as Maurice realized too late. He had assumed at Penge that a white-faced parson in a cassock could never have conceived of masculine love, but he knew now that there is no secret of humanity which, from a wrong angle, orthodoxy has not viewed, that religion is far more acute than science, and if it only added judgement to insight would be the greatest thing in the world. (221)

Is Maurice capable of such a generalized insight as, 'asceticism and piety have their practical side'? Does he really *know* that 'there is no secret of humanity which, from a wrong angle, orthodoxy has not viewed'? Obviously, if he were capable of such thoughts he would be closer to Forster than some of his words and actions, and Forster's avowed conception of him, declare him to be.

Stemming from Forster's uncertain attitude to Maurice are

passages of bathos in which style and assessment are disproportionate to the occasion. When Maurice realizes that he will
never have children, Forster tells us that 'an immense sadness'
rises up 'in his soul. He and the beloved would vanish utterly
– would continue neither in Heaven nor on Earth.' Such
cadenced and quasi-religious diction is inappropriate, even
more so when one recalls that Maurice is no longer a Christian. A similar sentimentality infuses Forster's appraisal of
Maurice's determination to sublimate his sexual urges by
working hard and helping others:

> He hadn't a God, he hadn't a lover – the two usual incentives to virtue. But
> on he struggled with his back to ease, because dignity demanded it. There
> was no one to watch him, nor did he watch himself, but struggles like his are
> the supreme achievements of humanity, and surpass any legends about
> Heaven. (132)

To call struggles like Maurice's the 'supreme achievements of
humanity' is not only sentimentally disproportionate; it is a
glaring sign of Forster's inability to detach himself from a hero,
whose self-pity too often projects his own.

III

Despite its flaws, *Maurice*, as Forster's only homosexual novel,
has a special importance: it suggests the extent to which
certain recurrent themes and incidents in his fiction are connected with his homosexual concerns. The journey theme, for
example, which takes the traveller from a world of middle-class
values and expectations to a new order of experience, would
seem to have some basis in Forster's discovery of his own
homosexuality – a discovery that Maurice's journey projects.
Moreover, the fact that so many of Forster's travellers become
involved, like Maurice, in tabooed relationships, leading in
some cases to scandalous revelations, can hardly be unconnected with Forster's awareness of the perils of being a homosexual. One thinks of Lilia's marriage to Gino; of Rickie's
discovery that Stephen, whom he despises, is his bastard half-
brother; of Helen's affair with Leonard Bast; and of Adela's

belief that she was assaulted by an Indian in a cave. Indeed, concerning Adela, the very selection of a cave as the site for her fantasy, together with Forster's evasiveness as to what exactly did happen in it, may reflect his understandable wish to keep his sexuality private.

Maurice also suggests the extent to which one of Forster's most persistent concerns, the divorce between the inner and outer life, must have been intensified by his homosexuality. As an adult trying to live in a 'normal' world, Maurice is made increasingly aware of a 'complete break between his public and private actions'. Should he follow the path of 'nature' or that of society? In *A Room with a View*, the choice is fairly clear-cut: Lucy must be guided by her emotions if she is to be saved. But by the time Forster came to the writing of *Howards End*, he obviously felt the desirability of trying to connect the subjective needs of the individual with the objective world of society; and to this end, he marries Margaret Schlegel, apostle of the inner life, to Henry Wilcox, the man of business. That the marriage seems forced and sterile, a yoking of opposites rather than a vital connection, may reflect Forster's underlying feeling that no vital connection was possible. Certainly *Maurice* suggests that, for the homosexual at least, it is not possible. Maurice would also like to connect his two worlds. '. . . the "life of the earth," he thinks, 'it ought to be the same as my daily life – the same society. One ought to be built on the other. . .' (200). But he finally learns that it cannot be: he can make no compromise; he must choose one or the other, and it is the 'life of the Earth' that he chooses.

Although he approves Maurice's choice, Forster's regard for nature is not naively romantic. Nature, as he often stresses, is unpredictable and indifferent to human needs. It gives Rickie a club foot, makes Maurice a homosexual, and turns Clive normal. As Maurice drives through the grounds at Penge, the flowers that he sees bring home to him the irony of his own condition:

Blossom after blossom crept past them, draggled by the ungenial year: some had cankered, others would never unfold: here and there beauty triumphed, but desperately, flickering in a world of gloom. Maurice looked into one after another, and though he did not care for flowers the failure irritated him. Scarcely anything was perfect. On one spray every flower was lopsided, the next swarmed with caterpillars, or bulged with galls. The indifference of nature! And her incompetence! (165)

That nature so often plays a sinister role in Forster's fiction may be partly attributable to his apprehension over his own sexuality, a condition that must have posed a constant threat to normal social relationships. When Maurice, walking in London, tries to reconcile his natural self with society's expectations and sees at the same time the sun sinking behind park trees, the vista melts into 'one huge creature that had fingers and fists of green' (200). A portentous symbol of how ruthlessly nature can dislocate mere social arrangements, it recalls the isolated ravine near Ravello where a party of picnickers in 'The Story of a Panic' are terrified by a visitation from Pan – the ravine 'a many-fingered green hand, palm upwards, which was clutching convulsively to keep us in its grasp'. The image also anticipates the 'fists and fingers' of the Marabar Hills – the setting for a sexual fantasy that does far more than discommode a party of picnickers.

A recurrent theme connected with nature's role, on which *Maurice* throws light, is the question of procreation. To have children, or not to have them: it is an issue on which several of Forster's key characters are sharply divided. Helen Schlegel loves her child by Leonard Bast; Margaret has no children and does not care for them. Neither does Fielding. 'I'd far rather leave a thought behind me than a child,' he tells Aziz,[5] who loves his children and is thankful that because of them his name will not die out. 'Why children?' Clive Durham asks. 'Why always children? For love to end where it begins is far more beautiful, and Nature knows it.' (88) But Maurice does not know it, and as we have seen is troubled by the sterility of homosexual love. Such a division among Forster's characters would seem to reflect the author's inability, or unwillingness, to settle the question for himself.

[5] *A Passage to India*, 119. Harcourt, Brace, New York, 1952.

A final point about *Maurice* is that the hero's retreat to the greenwood with Alec, where they will live together as 'outlaws', is in keeping with that note of alienation on which every one of the novels ends. Unable to marry Caroline and fed-up with Sawston, Philip Herriton goes off by himself to London. Rickie Elliot dies broken in spirit. Lucy's happiness at marrying George is clouded with the knowledge that she has alienated her family 'perhaps forever'. Removed from London and the rest of the Wilcox clan, Margaret and Henry vegetate in the country at Howards End. Aziz and Fielding are finally separated, spiritually and physically, by forces beyond their control. All such endings may indirectly express Forster's feeling that the needs of the homosexual are irreconcilable with the demands of society. 'Since *Maurice* was written,' he wrote in 1960,

there has been a change in the public attitude here: the change from ignorance and terror to familiarity and contempt. It is not the change towards which Edward Carpenter had worked. He had hoped for the generous recognition of an emotion and for the reintegration of something primitive into the common stock. And I, though less optimistic, had supposed that knowledge would bring understanding. (240)

If Forster had lived a generation later, he would, of course, have had ample ground for being less pessimistic. Had he been so, the tone and content of his fiction would doubtless have been much modified.

7

A Passage to India

In *Aspects of the Novel*, E. M. Forster remarks of *War and Peace* that when one has read it great chords begin to sound. Like all great works of art, Tolstoy's novel carries overtones richer and more suggestive than the literal significance of the elements that compose it. *A Passage to India* is no *War and Peace*: its range is narrower, its world less populous; yet from it too one may say that great chords reverberate. Its suggestive power is immense. It is unquestionably one of the great English novels, and the one novel of Forster's that fully justifies his reputation as a major twentieth-century novelist.

If it were only, as some early reviewers felt, an impressive piece of anti-colonial fiction, it would be little read today. But it has become a modern classic, as pertinent to our time as it was to the period between the two world wars, for it concerns no less a subject than man's attempt to find order and a basis for solid, durable values in our disordered and multifarious world. The India that Forster describes, with its multitudes of people, its races, creeds, and hierarchies, its conflicting aims and aspirations, is the modern world in epitome. How can the mind take hold of it? To what extent can purely human and personal values flourish in it? To what extent do man's attempts to achieve or discover order echo a cosmic or supernatural harmony? These are large and important questions; and because the novel deeply explores them in connection with characters and incidents that engage our sympathetic interest, it remains one of the most important novels of the century.

Forster's two lady travellers, Mrs Moore and Adela Quested, come to India expecting that though the country will prove exotic, it will confirm their belief that they live in an intelligible universe. In this belief, they are doomed to disappointment. Forster involves the two women in a series of situations that eventually undermines Mrs Moore's religious faith and hastens her death and leads Adela Quested to realize that the world is more mysterious and complicated than she had believed.

Mrs Moore is a Christian humanist with a touch of mysticism. Her universe is all of a piece, a uni-verse, and its God a God of love, who, as she explains to her son Ronny, 'has put us on earth to love our neighbours and to show it, and He is omnipresent, even in India, to see how we are succeeding' (51).[1] Looking up at the night sky soon after her arrival in Chandrapore, the fictitious town where most of the action is set, she feels a sudden, refreshing kinship with the moon and stars. Her approach to people is equally intuitive and direct. With none of the racial snobbery that characterizes most of the novel's Anglo-Indians, she can transcend the barriers that separate man from man, as witness her immediate friendship with Dr Aziz, whom near the beginning of the novel she meets outside a mosque.

Adela has little of Mrs Moore's intuitiveness and openness. A 'queer, cautious girl' (24), she is decent, inquisitive, and sexually inhibited, a combination virtually guaranteed in a Forster novel to lead its possessor into a first-class muddle. The world, she believes, is susceptible to observation and intelligent inquiry; and in the spirit of this belief, she wants to see 'the real India'. Understandably, as she herself declares, she dislikes mystery, for mystery by definition baffles the rational understanding and violates her belief that everything is, in theory at least, comprehensible. Mrs Moore, on the other hand, dislikes muddle, which violates her vision of an orderly Christian cosmos (69).

The India that Forster delineates, however, is both muddled and mysterious. Its equivocal character is suggested in its very landscape. This landscape has two aspects, fertile and dry, the former predominating in the first and third parts of the novel ('Mosque' and 'Temple'), the latter in the second ('Caves').

[1] All references to pages in *A Passage to India* are to the Harcourt, Brace, New York, 1952 edition.

The tropical trees that soar over Chandrapore, the flowers whose scent is carried to Aziz as he sits outside the mosque, the mangoes and water chestnut in Fielding's garden, the floods at Mau, and the parklike setting in which Aziz and Fielding ride together, all suggest a land richly fertile. But here and there in the first part, a more sinister aspect is injected, a reminder that the world is not always benign and a foreshadowing of Adela's and Mrs Moore's experience in the Marabar Hills. A vulture and some kites soar over the British club during the Bridge Party. From the apparent safety of the club grounds, Adela peers through a nick in a cactus hedge at the 'fists and fingers' of the Marabar Hills. Flies infest Aziz's dwelling, a mysterious animal collides with the Nawabab Bahadur's car, leopards and snakes are common in the surrounding country, and with the approach of summer there is dust and sickness. The sun, which can 'rain glory into the Chandrapore bazaars' (9), becomes toward the end of the 'Mosque' part destructively hot, the emblem of a universe that blindly creates, preserves, and destroys its life. The Ganges that flows from Vishnu's foot through Siva's hair is a river of life and death, the same water that irrigates the land depositing mud and filth, and harbouring crocodiles that devour the dead bodies borne down from Benares. 'What a terrible river! What a wonderful river!' exclaims Mrs Moore (32). Chandrapore, as Forster describes it in the opening chapter, seems, apart from the anomalous civil station, an organic extension of the river, a microcosm in which life, death and continuity mirror the universal process. 'Houses do fall, people are drowned and left rotting, but the general outline of the town persists, swelling here, shrinking there, like some low but indestructible form of life.' (7) The landscape of the Marabar Hills when Aziz, Adela and Mrs Moore visit it at the start of summer is baked and cactus-ridden, a land suggestive of sickness and death. To the visitors, everything seems 'infected with illusion' (140). What looks like a snake turns out to be a withered stump – or perhaps, as Aziz suggests, a snake after all. The sunrise 'trailing yellowish behind the trees' (137–8), the sky itself 'unhealthily near' (141), the surrounding granite 'dead and quiet' (141), the mud, the cactus, and the dark, claustral caves, all seem elements of a tainted land. Even the train returning to Chandrapore looks like 'a coffin from the scientific north', whose passengers resemble 'corpses' (161).

Life-sustaining and life-denying, blending tropical luxuriance with mud, cactus, flies, snakes, leopards, hyenas, and dust, the landscape of Forster's India defies man's instinct for order and clarity. The very mud that cakes Chandrapore seems redolent of muddle. Small wonder that Mrs Moore, whose cosmic vision was nourished by the English Lake District, feels acutely uneasy in India.

The bewildering character of the country provokes from Forster himself an evasiveness that occasionally makes it difficult to assess his attitude and interpret his meaning. His treatment of Mrs Moore's experience in the Marabar cave is a case in point. On the one hand he describes her vision as if it is a valid insight into ultimate truth; on the other, he undercuts it with the laconic aside, 'Visions are supposed to entail profundity, but – Wait till you get one, dear reader!' (208) A comment about Mr Turton's decision to give a bridge party is equally ambiguous. 'All invitations,' we are told, 'must proceed from heaven perhaps; perhaps it is futile for men to initiate their own unity, they do but widen the gulfs between them by the attempt.' Then, as if the two 'perhases' were insufficient to convey the author's wish not to commit himself on the matter too definitely, Forster proceeds to detach himself from it altogether by continuing – 'So at all events though old Mr Graysford and young Mr Sorely, the devoted missionaries who lived out beyond the slaughterhouses, always travelled third on the railways, and never came up to the club.' These two devoted missionaries are then subjected to a paragraph of gentle ridicule that completely sabotages the original observation, whether theirs or Forster's, that 'all invitations must proceed from heaven perhaps' (38). Such ambiguities reflect, I think, Forster's abiding sense of life's complexities and his refusal to be content with easy generalizations.

In such a country as India, what visible suggestion is there of a unified cosmos guided by a Divine Providence? Only the overarching sky that seems to enclose the world in a protective curve, and from which at night the same stars shine as one sees over England. It is the sky's curve and familiar stars that facilitate Mrs Moore's cosy feeling of oneness with the universe.

But her feeling, as Forster again and again implies and as she herself soon begins to realize, is based on wishful thinking. The novel is everywhere pervaded with a sense that we inhabit a universe beyond which is only darkness and nothing. In chapter 1, for example, Forster's description of the sky clearly suggests this. 'The core of blue,' we are told, 'persists, and so it is by night. Then the stars hang like lamps from the immense vault. The distance between the vault and them is as nothing to the distance behind them, and that farther distance, though beyond colour, last freed itself from blue.' (9) Mrs Moore's speech to Ronny about God's omnipresence and love is qualified by the disquieting thought that 'Outside the arch there seemed always an arch, beyond the remotest echo a silence.' (52) When Adela and Ronny take a car ride into the country one night, the darkness seems 'to well out of the meagre vegetation'. And when the car goes over a bump, causing their hands to touch in a 'spurious unity', Forster portentously observes that 'the darkness is alone durable' (88). After Fielding's tea-party, Mrs Moore drily remarks to her son that she is 'pledged to nothing' (82), a prophecy ironically fulfilled by her eventual spiritual nihilism. 'Nothing,' declares Aziz, 'embraces the whole of India, nothing, nothing' (145); by which he presumably means that India is not one but multiple and that no creed or vision can fully express it. But his words also suggest that India is literally embraced by *nothing* – that it is part of a universe beyond which is nothing, a universe without any purpose or justification beyond its own existence.

That the universe may be without ulterior meaning and value is conveyed through the richest and most elusive of Forster's natural symbols, the Marabar Caves. The hills that

6-2

house them suggest primordial chaos, for they are 'older than all spirit', 'without the proportion that is kept by the wildest hills elsewhere', perhaps even 'flesh of the sun's flesh' (123). When Aziz tries to learn from Godbole the reason for the Marabar's reputation, he gets nowhere, his 'comparatively simple mind' encountering 'Ancient Night' (76), that Miltonic and classical deity who with Chaos ruled the unformed region between heaven and hell. It is into this region that Mrs Moore psychologically retreats after her trip to the caves when, in a state of 'spiritual muddledom', she comes to a 'twilight of the double vision' in which she can 'neither act nor refrain from action...neither ignore nor respect infinity'. Forster's association of the caves with Ancient Night and by implication with Chaos is in keeping with his insistence that whatever had spoken to Mrs Moore in their depths was 'before time' and 'before space' (207–8). Identical in size and structure and virtually indistinguishable from one another, the caves baffle man's instinct for order – a fact that Ronny, with typical impercipience, fails to recognize when he declares that the Government intends to number them in sequence with white paint to prevent future incidents (199).

Untenanted the caves are valueless, for 'nothing, nothing attaches to them' (124) Unlike Plato's celebrated cave into which the sunlight penetrated to cast shadows on the walls, the Marabar Caves are dark. Their value depends on what one brings into them. A flame reflected in the highly polished walls of the chamber gives forth lovely iridescent colours before its light expires and darkness again takes over (125). What does the flame signify? Beauty undoubtedly, but also man's desire for harmony and for union with a sympathetic alter-ego, or as Shelley called it, with 'a soul of one's soul'. When Aziz meets Mrs Moore for the first time, 'the flame that not even beauty can nourish' springs up in his heart (23). The friends who call on him when he is ill emanate 'little ineffectual unquenchable flames' (107). And when Ronny and Adela hold hands in the Nawab Bhadur's car, their warmth is as 'local and temporary as the gleam that inhabits a firefly' (88). The light reflected in the walls of the chamber is a visual echo, a projected symbol, of man's desire for beauty and unity.

But the same walls that reflect the light from a match also have a remarkable power to echo sound; and no matter what sound the visitor emits, the echo is always the same – 'boum'. 'Hope, politeness, the blowing of a nose, the squeak of a boot, all produce "boum".' (147) Obviously, Forster is straining physical plausibility to make a symbolic point, the point I take it being that all value is ultimately subjective and, under the eye of eternity, equally meaningless. Man yearns for some transcendent confirmation of the values that he himself imposes upon his experience, but like Narcissus all he receives are echoes of his desires. No longer is there a solid, objective basis for whatever order man assures or imposes upon society, a fact that Fielding comes to realize, but Ronny does not. Apropos the blow to British administration caused by the trip to the caves, Fielding thinks to himself, 'We all build upon sand; and the more modern the country gets, the worse'll be the crash. In the old eighteenth century, when cruelty and injustice raged, an invisible power repaired their ravages. Everything echoes now; there's no stopping the echo.' (276) But Ronny, tacitly assuming that his 'superiority' to the natives is simply a manifestation of some natural, God-given order, calls angrily to his peon Krishna to bring the files, only to be answered by the echoes of his own egotistical promptings. 'Krishna the earth, Krishna the stars replied, until the Englishman was appeased by their echoes, fined the absent peon eight annas, and sat down to his arrears in the next room.' (97)

As to the caves' echoes themselves, one point should be stressed: they appear to make a devastating impression on only two of the characters, Mrs Moore and Adela. The servants and villagers in the cave with Mrs Moore do not seem to be troubled by them. Professor Godbole, who knows the caves well, does not mention an echo when he describes them at Fielding's tea-party. 'It never impressed him, perhaps.' (147) Shouting into a cave for Adela, Aziz hears the echo, but there is no sign that it disturbs him. Fielding, who arrives by car at the site, having missed the train, runs up to a cave just to see one, but is not 'impressed' (158).

Now Godbole, Aziz, and Fielding are three very dissimilar people, but they have one thing in common: they are sure of their spiritual values and insights and act accordingly. Whatever their limitations, they are not muddled. Mrs Moore and Adela, on the other hand, are. They have been undergoing a spiritual crisis almost since their arrival in India; for Mrs Moore a crisis of faith, for Adela a crisis of conduct. Under the impress of India, Mrs Moore begins to doubt whether her simple Christian faith can adequately comprehend the muddle and mystery around her. Her doubt is heightened at Fielding's tea-party by the strange song that Professor Godbole sings, the 'Song of an Unknown Bird'. 'I will explain in detail,' says Godbole after he has sung:

'It was a religious song. I placed myself in the position of a milk-maiden. I say to Shri Krishna, "Come! come to me only." The god refuses to come. I grow humble and say: "Do not come to me only. Multiply yourself into a hundred companions, but one, O Lord of the Universe, come to me." He refuses to come. This is repeated several times. The song is composed in a raga appropriate to the present hour, which is the evening.'

'But He comes in some other song, I hope?' said Mrs Moore gently.

'Oh no, he refuses to come,' repeated Godbole, perhaps not understanding her question. 'I say to Him, Come, come come, come, come, come. He neglects to come.' (80)

Nagged then with a sense of a non-personal God, or perhaps of no God at all, and feeling 'bottled up' by the heat, Mrs Moore goes into a cave and experiences an intensification of her mood, a horrible claustrophobia (there are crowds of villagers in the cave as well) and the sound of the echo. The fact that it terrifies her reflects her spiritual muddledom. Coming upon her when she is tired and doubtful, it seems to murmur, 'Pathos, piety, courage – they exist, but are identical, and so is filth. Everything exists, nothing has value.' (149) Under the spell of the echo her former Christian optimism crumbles. She becomes cynical and withdrawn, taking no further interest in human affairs, and wishing only to be left alone, to retire 'into a cave of my own...where no young people will come asking questions and expecting answers' (200).

Two points should be made about Mrs Moore's 'vision' in the cave. The first is that though it is a result of muddledom and exhaustion, it is fully in accord with the novel's recurrent implication that man's values are without transcendent sanction.

The second point would hardly need to be made were it not that many readers have seen Mrs Moore's 'vision' as analogous to the ultimate insight of the Hindu mystic, the merging of Brahman and Atman, of Self and Non-Self, in which value itself is annihilated. F. C. Crews, in one of the best studies of Forster's fiction, more convincingly maintains the opposite. Mrs Moore's vision, he says, is rather an anti-vision, a kind of parodic inversion of the Hindu mystic's perception. 'Instead of blending her identity with that of the world-soul, she reduces the world-soul to the scale of her own wearied ego; her dilettantish yearning for oneness with the universe has been echoed, not answered.'[2]

Just as the echo is an objective correlative for Mrs Moore's crisis of faith, so is it the same for Adela's crisis of conduct. Unable to decide whether to marry Ronny, whom she does not really love, she has also become muddled. At Fielding's tea party, she impulsively tells Aziz and Godbole, before she has said anything on the subject to Ronny, that she does not intend to remain in India. Later she breaks off her engagement, only to renew it during the car ride with Ronny, aroused as she is by her physical contact with him. Nevertheless, she remains unsure of herself. 'I feel I haven't been – frank enough, attentive enough, or something,' she tells Mrs Moore. 'It's as if I got everything out of proportion...I meant to be good when I sailed, but somehow I haven't been.' (98) Like Lucy Honeychurch, she has failed to face honestly her own desires and instincts, and so suffers that favourite Forsterian malady, muddle; a muddle that the caves simply objectify. Her

[2] Frederick C. Crewe, *E. M. Forster: The Perils of Humanism*, p. 159. Princeton, 1967.

entry into a cave is both a physical and a psychological step. In Jungian terms, the shadow that she sees and at which in vain she strikes with her binoculars (an instrument intended to clarify vision, not compound confusion) is her own – her repressed instinctual life now rising up to confront her rational Self. The echo – the echo of her own confusion – rages up and down her nerves until, at Aziz's trial, she courageously searches her own conscience, and, realizing that her accusation was only a cloak to screen her confusion, declares Aziz innocent. Then and only then can she truthfully say, as she does to Fielding, 'I have no longer any secrets. My echo is gone.' (239)

Considered objectively, the hills and caves suggest a disordered universe in which man nevertheless tries to discover order, and to order his own life accordingly. Their round echoing chambers echo the curving sky, beyond which lies for Christian, Moslem, and Hindu an inspiring vision of eternity. But the chambers, the novel suggests, are the reality; the universe leading to heaven, hell, nirvana, or what you will, only a projection of man's desire.

Subjectively viewed, the caves are psychological. Each man, enclosed in his own cave, tries to reach out and commune with his fellow man; but the caves separate man from man, keeping each in his own compartment, discouraging intimacy between Moslem and Hindu, English and Indian, white man and dark, high caste and low. The echo that terrifies Mrs Moore and rages up and down Adela's nerves extends to the world beyond, for it, too, with its mixture of races, creeds, and classes exemplifies spiritual muddledom.

No doubt the caves and echoes are too suggestive. Forster strains physical plausibility to imply with their aid too much. They muddle the reader as well as the casual visitor. Nevertheless, their general intent is clear – to point to the problems that confront man when he tries to chart a course in a disordered world.

It is these problems that Forster is concerned to explore in *A Passage to India*, and to explore them under three interrelated aspects, the religious, the social–political, and the personal. The exploration is an ironic one for it stems from the author's sustained perception that all order that man envisions or achieves is at best partial and temporary, at worst spurious.

Each of the three major religions of the novel, Christianity, Islam, and Hinduism, assumes some sort of metaphysical order underlying and informing the phenomenal world. Each endows 'the unseen' with value and purports to express man's relationship with it. And each, in Forster's view, is in its own way inadequate.

Christianity assumes an all-loving God, who shares our moral ideals, hears our prayers, and is concerned about our lives. Narrowly practised as in Forster's Anglo-India, it is exclusive rather than inclusive, a kind of churchy counterpart of the British club, and forced, as Mr Sorley, the devoted missionary admits, to exclude someone from its gathering or be left with nothing. The god of Anglo-India is he who saves the King, supports the police, and blesses the British Empire.

Mrs Moore's Christianity, of course, is purer. Transcending the narrowness of one particular creed, it is essentially a religion of love heightened by a mystical sense of the divine. It enables Mrs Moore to bridge the barrier of race and creed and make friends with Aziz. And yet, as she soon comes to realize, it cannot comprehend India's muddle, the heat, the sickness, the masses of humanity 'grading and drifting beyond the educated vision' (37). Her sense of kinship with the heavenly bodies was too easy: it left too much of the universe out of account.

Islam the religion of Dr Aziz, one of Forster's most attractive characters, is more sympathetically treated. Less amenable than Christianity to nationalistic bias, it appeals to Aziz's sense of beauty and history, enabling him to write sentimental poetry glorifying the Islamic past. But what relevance has it to the needs of the present? 'Of what help in this latitude and hour are the glories of Cordova and Samarcand?' asks Aziz. 'They have gone, and while we lament them the English occupy Delhi and exclude us from East Africa. Islam itself, though true, throws cross-lights over the path to freedom. The song of the future must transcend creed.' (268) Mosques may be beautiful; they may refresh and inspire the devout; but Forster's own judgment of them is explicit: '...those shallow arcades' provide 'but a limited asylum. "There is no God but God" doesn't carry us far through the complexities of matter and spirit; it is only a game with words, really, a religious pun, not a religious truth.' (276)

As for Hinduism, it comes closer than either Islam or Christianity to expressing and comprehending the monumental confusions of Indian life. The great temple-scene with its cacophonic mixture of music, noise, revelry, and mystical piety, seems a veritable apotheosis of India's muddle and mystery. Not by accident Forster has placed the scene immediately after his account of Fielding's arrival in Venice. For Venice, unlike India, exemplifies 'the civilization that has escaped muddle, the spirit in a reasonable form, with flesh and blood subsisting' (282). In Venice, everything is placed right; all is harmony. At Mau there is 'a frustration of reason and form' (285). But Venice's beauty as Forster describes it, is that of art, a Venice without life or movement, a Canaletto view, not the living reality. The spirit of Mau, on the other hand, is the spirit of life: all is life and movement.

Some jumped in the air, others flung themselves prone and embraced the bare feet of the universal lover; the women behind the purdah slapped and shrieked; the little girl slipped out and danced by herself, her black pigtails flying. Not an orgy of the body; the tradition of that shrine forbade it. But the human spirit had tried by a desperate contortion to ravish the unknown, flinging down science and history in the struggle, yes, beauty herself. (288)

To which does Forster owe his allegiance, to the spirit of art as symbolized by Venice or to that of life as symbolized by Mau? To both, of course; and his main task as a human being and novelist is to reconcile them.

In *The Hill of Devi*, Forster describes the festival of Gokul Ashtami – the event that inspired the last section of *A Passage to India* – and the description illuminates his attitude to Hinduism in general. 'What troubles me,' he writes, is that every detail, almost without exception, is fatuous and in bad taste. The altar is a mess of little objects, stifled with rose leaves, the walls are hung with deplorable oleographs, the chandaliers, draperies, everything bad. Only one thing is beautiful – the expression on the faces of the people as they bow to the shrine... There is no dignity, no taste, no form, and though I am dressed as a Hindu I shall never become one. I don't think one ought to be irritated with Idolatry because one can see from the faces of the people that it touches something very deep in their hearts. But it is natural that Missionaries, who think these ceremonies wrong as well as inartistic, should lose their tempers.[3]

The Dionysian spirit of the festival points to what for Forster would be a signal deficiency of Hinduism, its comparative unconcern for the welfare of individuals so far as their life on earth is concerned. Godbole, the chief embodiment of the Hindu spirit in the novel, is no humanist. As his name suggests, he loves God, not people – not, at any rate, for themselves. He may have a deep and subtle mind – though Forster gives no convincing evidence that he does – but toward people he is completely detached, appearing both friendless and unbefriendable. Thus at Fielding's tea-party he sits apart, more of a curiosity than a companion, displaying a complete incapacity for ordinary conversation. Either through negligence or design, he misses the train to the Marabar Caves, causes Fielding to miss it too, and thereby contributes to the ensuing catastrophe. When Fielding asks his opinion as to Aziz's guilt or innocence, his reply, that 'when evil occurs, it expresses the whole universe', may or may not be true, but it reflects no concern for either Aziz or Fielding. His mind is preoccupied with what is for him a more pressing matter: what should he name the new school that he intends to open at Mau? Presiding over the festival at Mau, he remembers an old woman, Mrs Moore, 'though she was not important to him', and impels her 'by his spiritual force to that place where completeness can be found'. Rapt in meditation, he loves 'all men, the whole universe' (286); but it is an utterly impersonal love, the love of a saint or mystic for the Divine, not of one human being for another. Godbole's otherworldliness recalls that which Forster attributed to Dante in his early essay on the

[3] *The Hill of Devi*, 107. Arnold, 1953.

Italian poet; and the point that Forster made in that essay concerning Dante's rarified love for Beatrice could well be applied to Godbole's love for man. Which, asks Forster, pays the truer homage – 'Dante looking through Beatrice, or Othello looking at Desdemona; Dante narrating the return of his lady to the angels, or King Lear with Cordelia dead in his arms?'⁴ And which, he might equally have asked, pays the truer homage, the friendship of Fielding and Aziz, or Godbole's love of 'all men, the whole universe'? (286)

Some readers have regarded Godbole with the respect that Hindus would normally accord an elderly Brahman. Forster, however, generally treats him with gentle satire. When Fielding asks his opinion as to what might really have happened in the Marabar Caves, Godbole's reply is punctuated with actions calculated to render him slightly ridiculous. He 'sucked in his thin cheeks...He stopped again...Now he had an air of daring and of coyness...He looked shyly down the sleeve of his own coat.' (178) And he concludes his metaphysical explanation of evil with a not clearly relevant story about a Hindu Rajah who atoned for killing his nephew by giving a thirsty cow a drink of water. 'Professor Godbole's conversations frequently culminated in a cow. Fielding received this one in gloomy silence.' (179) At the festival, his pince-nez askew (it had caught in a jasmine garland) and singing into his colleague's moustache, Godbole is at once impressive and ludicrous, an embodiment of the very qualities that Forster, in *The Hill of Devi*, perceives in the festival of Gokul Ashtami. As a Brahman priest, Godbole helps to perpetuate the Hindu caste-system, which in itself does nothing to alleviate the hunger and social degradation in which millions of Indians are placed. *A Passage to India* pays little heed to these millions; for they are beyond the range of Forster's 'educated vision'; but there is no question that Hinduism's own incapacity to help them would limit its human value and validity. With its gaze

⁴ 'Dante', *The Working Men's College Journal*, vol. 10 (February-April 1908), 264. Reprinted in *Albergo Empedocle and Other Writings*, ed. G. H. Thomson, 151 (New York, 1971).

fixed on a hypothetical hereafter, it neglects the values of the present; and no religion that does that would have satisfied Forster. 'Will it really profit us so much,' he asks in *The Longest Journey*, 'if we save our souls and lose the whole world?'

So far, as this world goes, man tries to order his life in and through society, and the societies that he creates are expressions of his instinct for order. *A Passage to India* presents two antithetically opposed social orders: that which the English try to impose on India and that which the Indians have evolved themselves. Anglo-Indian order is, from Forster's point of view, bad because it is utterly alien and imposed without regard for the needs and values of the Indians themselves. Ronny Heaslop puts the British attitude beyond doubt when he tells his mother, 'We're not pleasant in India, and we don't intend to be pleasant. We've something more important to do.' (50) The British, as Forster presents them, try to rule with a certain machine-like efficiency. Not that the best of them are inhumane (and Forster is careful to show that not all are utterly unsympathetic to Indian feelings) but they are all caught by the system – even, eventually, Fielding. Native societies, on the other hand, for all their failure to afford more than a handful of Indians a decent chance in life, are at least indigenous and organic. Rather than being imposed on India, they have evolved out of it, and in this sense may be regarded as a complex embodiment of the spirit of place. That Forster has always had a deep-seated distrust of any order forcibly imposed is shown by numerous passages in his writings, among them his account in *The Longest Journey* of Sawston School and its rigid administrator Herbert Pembroke. Anglo-Indian order like that of Sawston is doomed because it strives to suppress the essentially disorderly life force. 'The triumphant machine of civilization,' warns Forster, 'may suddenly hitch and be immobilized into a car of stone...' (211)

Forster contrasts the two concepts of order, the British and Indian, through an appropriate choice of symbols. The neat, arid civil station with its roads intersecting at right angles conveys the orderly mind of Anglo-India. Arches and circles help to express the Indian sense of order. The red-brick bungalows and roads have no symbolic kinship with anything in nature; they are objects imposed upon it. Arches and circles, however, imitate the sky's concavity, which contributes so strongly to man's sense of an orderly universe. The 'shallow arcades' of the mosque and the Minto, the three arches of painted blue wood that open out into Fielding's garden, the dome in the Shrine of the Head at Mau, the legendary mountain 'that turned into an umbrella', and the bubble-shaped cave rumoured to lie within the boulder atop Kawa Dol, all derive their ultimate inspiration from the curve of the sky. Indian society, as Forster appears to conceive it, is composed of innumerable circles. Aziz and his friends inhabit a small Moslem one; Aziz's colleague Dr Pann Lal a Hindu one; and except when professional need demands it, the two circles seldom touch. Hamidullah Begum tells of a noble woman who inhabits such a 'narrow circle' that she can find no husband and is bound to die unwed. India's circles include everyone, even those 'drifting beyond the educated vision' whom 'no earthly invitation can embrace'. In a seemingly ritualistic parody, Ronny's servants respond to his angry summons by running 'slowly in circles, carrying hurricane lamps', imitating as it were the indifferent sky whose 'echoes' eventually appease the Englishman (97).

All social order, however, whether imposed or evolving, is fragile, liable like the boulder on Kawa Dol to fall and smash, and reveal its hollowness. If Indian society is intrinsically superior to the order that Anglo-India strives to impose on it, it is because it is vital and changeable, a complex of orders paradoxically accommodating disorder, and disorder is as vital to human happiness as its opposite. Perhaps, from Forster's particular point of view, more vital. 'Speaking as a writer,' he declares in 'Art for Art's Sake', 'What I hope for today is a disorder which will be more favourable to artists than is the present one...there have been some advantageous disorders in the past...and we may do something to accelerate the next one.'

Social organization is one expression of man's instinct for order; love and friendship, or what Forster calls personal relationships, another. 'Starting from them,' he writes in 'What I Believe', 'I get a little order into the contemporary chaos.' *A Passage to India* is in part the story of three personal relationships, all of which, under the force of circumstances largely beyond the control of the individuals concerned, disintegrate. Aziz's friendship with Mrs Moore necessarily dies with Mrs Moore's death. His friendship with Fielding suffers an apparently irreparable breach when the latter, after Aziz's trial, treats Adela considerately and tries to persuade Aziz not to sue her for disproportionate damages. Adela's engagement to Ronny, which was never more than a lukewarm liason, is broken forever by her conduct at the trial. In all three relationships, the forces that make for separation finally outweigh those that draw people together. Man's quest for order, the novel suggests, whether expressed through personal relationships, social organization, or religious vision, is at best partial and precarious. The forces that drive men into compartments are an ever-present threat. Moreover, whatever order man does manage to achieve can afford but a limited shelter in a disordered universe.

Forster's sense of ultimate disorder is underlined by the novel's structure. In great part it consists of a linked series of episodes, each of which expresses an attempt to achieve order but which inevitably disintegrates into its opposite, though generally not before preparing the way for the next episode. Taken in its entirety, this series not only helps to define the novel's structure, it is the dominant element in its rhythm. Aziz's meeting with Mrs Moore is the key link in the series, for from it grow most of the other important scenes and encounters. It leads to the so-called Bridge Party, Mr Turton's effort to enable his two visitors to meet Indians. Uninspired by genuine goodwill to the Indians, the party is doomed from the start, such harmony as it achieves being purely formal. The English form one group, the Indians another, and conversation between the races is limited to polite vacuities. When Mrs

Moore and Adela try to converse with a Hindu couple, the
Bhattacharyas, the comedy reaches its climax:

'I wonder whether you would allow us to call on you some day.'
   'When?' she [Mrs Bhattacharya] replied charmingly.
   'Whenever is convenient.'
   'All days are convenient.'
   'Thursday...'
   'Most certainly.'
   'We shall enjoy it greatly, it would be a real pleasure. What about the time?'
   'All hours.'
   'Tell us which you would prefer. We're quite strangers to your country;
we don't know when you have visitors,' said Miss Quested.
   Mrs Bhattacharya seemed not know either. Her gesture implied that she
had known, since Thursdays began, that English ladies would come to see
her on one of them, and so always stayed in. Everything pleased her, nothing
surprised. She added, 'We leave for Calcutta to-day.'
   'Oh, do you?' said Adela, not at first seeing the implication. Then she cried,
'Oh, but if you do we shall find you gone.' Mrs Bhattacharya did not dispute
it.

All concerned are barricaded within their separate caves and
can get nowhere. A 'shapeless discussion' ensues and the party
ends, though not before Fielding takes the opportunity to
invite the two women to his house to tea to meet Aziz and
Professor Godbole.

Being smaller and inspired by goodwill, the tea-party is
more promising than the bridge party and, despite a small but
portentous misunderstanding between Aziz and Fielding, gets
off to a good start. But Godbole turns out to be as impenetrable
to genuine communication as the Bhattacharyas were. Like
them he embodies the mysterious side of India which, together
with its muddle, confounds the travellers' expectations. His
'Song of the Unknown Bird' is not simply about the god who
refuses to come when prayed to; it is about the elusiveness of
India itself. With Ronny's untimely entrance, comparative
harmony gives way to muddle. Ronny is rude and superior.
Irritations mount, and the party disintegrates.

In the meantime, the trip to the caves has been prepared for.
Designed by Aziz – though without irony – as 'a stupendous
replica of the tea party' (126), it turns out to be just that. Order

and harmony are threatened at the start when Godbole and Fielding fail to appear. The heat of the sun aggravates the threat, but the bond between the three principals is enough to keep order until Mrs Moore and Adela enter their respective caves. At this point, disintegration begins, then spreads like an epidemic through Chandrapore. Aziz's trial is a last effort to restore order. Perhaps the most effectively comic scene in the novel, it shows the British vainly juggling with order and precedence until, with Adela's testimony, the whole 'flimsy framework' of the court breaks up and only the man with the punkah is left to agitate the swirling clouds of dust descending onto the overturned furniture. Like the servitor in the Mau tank, impassively viewing the overturned boats and their floundering occupants, he serves as a timeless reminder of the ultimate vanity of all human attempts to achieve order. Following the trial, disorder sets in until a new set of administrators takes over.

The last part of the novel, marking a break in the action, is set in the native state of Mau about two years later. Whatever else it conveys, the festival that dominates the action illustrates the possibility of achieving a vital harmony, one, that is, that fully accommodates man's desire for disorder. The participants are both one and multiple, each self-directed, yet part of a whole dedicated to the celebration of Krishna's birth. Under the spell of Gokul Ashtami, Aziz renews his friendship with Fielding and makes friends with Ralph Moore. But the harmony cannot be sustained forever. The festival itself expresses an ecstasy that must of its very nature pass. Aziz must go one way, Fielding another, and the novel ends on a disintegrating note:

'Why can't we be friends now?' said the other [Fielding], holding him affectionately. 'It's what I want. It's what you want.'

But the horses didn't want it – they swerved apart; the earth didn't want it, sending up rocks through which riders must pass single file; the temples, the tank, the jail, the palace, the birds, the carrion, the Guest House, that came into view as they issued from the gap and saw Mau beneath: they didn't want it, they said in their hundred voices, 'No, not yet,' and the sky said, 'No, not there.' (322)

If *A Passage to India* reflected only the negative gospel that all human attempts to achieve order and unity are bound in the end to fail in a meaningless and chaotic universe, it would be a depressing book indeed. But that it is not in the least depressing, most readers, I think, would agree. And the chief reason that it is not depressing is that, despite its metaphysical and sociological implications, it communicates a sense that life is valuable for its own sake. For all Fielding's gloomy assertion that 'everything echoes now', everything emphatically does not echo. When Mrs Moore passes through Central India on her way to Bombay, she sees things totally unconnected with her experiences in Chandrapore and the Marabar Hills. The landscape, though 'baked and bleached', is not melancholy. The houses and temples give evidence of 'the indestructible life of man' (209). The fortress at Asirgarh has a solidity that belies her 'twilight of the double vision' (207). There is after all, as she realizes with a tinge of regret, so much of India that she will never see, so much that is alien to her own experience of the country, and she longs to 'disentangle the hundred Indias' that pass her in the streets of Bombay (210). The waving palms lining the harbour seem to her to be saying, 'So you thought an echo was India; you took the Marabar caves as final?...What have we in common with them, or they with Asirgarh? Good-bye!' Surely the entire passage, taken in conjunction with Mrs Moore's experience in the Marabar Hills, points to the contrast between a world infused with vitality and variety and one that her world-weary soul has reduced to a meaningless boum. The world may indeed be disordered and meaningless, but it still exists and must be experienced for its own sake. The cow, as Ansell insists in *The Longest Journey*, is there. The abyss that Mrs Moore sees may be there – an ultimate nothingness that opposes all life, all human effort, all love; but the life, the effort, and the love continue: they have their own validity and strength, like the palm trees that wave good-bye.

Unlike some writers, Forster does not view life as futile and meaningless, and none of his characters are emblems of futility. Even Mrs Moore, who succumbs to a nihilistic despair, has been a positive force, committed to the belief that life is worthwhile in itself. Fielding's 'I want to go on living a bit' and Adela's 'So do I' express the dominant view (264). Neither Fielding nor Aziz succumbs to the destructive forces around him. Neither becomes disordered nor disoriented. Aziz casts his lot with Indian nationalism, Fielding with Anglo-India, but both remain committed to the belief that life, friendship, and human brotherhood are worth the effort. So despite the novel's negative implications, it is emphatically not a negative book. It communicates a sense of the power and value of life, and of the possibilities that perenially exist for human beings to search for meaning and to express themselves through their institutions, art, and friendships. Though no order is all-embracing, though only the darkness is durable, the world is still ours, a forum for man's creative energies, an inexhaustible theatre in which to build and enjoy life.

Conclusion

I

To what extent, it must finally be asked, does Forster's fiction reflect the literary conventions and social conditions of a bygone era, and to what extent does it transcend that era and speak to us?

Unquestionably all of the fiction, not excluding *A Passage to India* and the posthumously published short stories – most of them written after 1920 – reflects a cultural climate that existed before the First World War and radically changed afterwards. Lucy Honeychurch visiting Florence with her chaperon, Philip Herriton with his snobbish and superficial aestheticism, and Rickie Elliot writing mythological tales about Pans and dryads, belong to a world that has gone. The sheltered life of the Schlegel sisters seems almost as remote from that of the modern woman as that of Emma Woodhouse and Elizabeth Bennet. In today's world Maurice could have been an active and happy homosexual as well as a stockbroker. Even *A Passage to India*, Forster's best and most socially comprehensive novel, deals with a colonialism on its way out when the novel appeared. When Forster was asked why he had written no more novels after *A Passage to India*, he replied that he felt too out-of-step with the postwar world to convey its climate. His postwar fiction generally supports this contention. His world is essentially Edwardian and early Georgian.

In its technique Forster's fiction is also early modern, in some respects pre-modern. Unlike James, Conrad, Joyce and Lawrence, Forster did little to extend the scope of the novel as a medium of imaginative expression. He was no innovator. In his readiness to comment upon his characters and to philosophize about the human condition, he is more akin to Victorian novelists like Dickens and Thackeray than to that aloof impersonal artist extolled by Stephen Dedalus. A highly personal writer, Forster projects himself into his fiction, and though his views and values may be sometimes hard to pin down, his personality marks everything he writes.

His affinities with Jane Austen have often been noticed, and Forster himself has acknowledged her influence. 'I learned from her the possibilities of domestic humour,' he has said.[1] And indeed his tea-parties and 'bridge parties' and outings to Fiesole and to Madingley recall analogous social events in her novels. Such characters as Miss Bartlett, Herbert Pembroke, Mrs Herriton, and the Anglo-Indian wives in *A Passage to India* could, allowing for superficial changes, fit into Jane Austen's world. Like her, he tends to focus upon the moneyed and leisured upper-middle-class, the modern equivalent of her gentry; and like her, he shows little capacity for dealing with the ill-fed, ill-housed, and ill-educated – those who perhaps constitute a majority of the human race. His declaration in *Howards End*, 'We are not concerned with the very poor. They are unthinkable',[2] perhaps consciously echoes the beginning of the last chapter of *Mansfield Park*: 'Let other pens dwell on guilt and misery. I quit such odious subjects as soon as I can.' Howards End recalls the great houses in Jane Austen's novels; and Margaret Schlegel's 'triumph' in marrying Henry and becoming its mistress parallels Elizabeth Bennet's in marrying Darcy and becoming mistress of Pemberley. Both women must overcome an initial prejudice against the men they are destined to marry.

Nevertheless, for all its affinities with the fiction of earlier writers, Forster's is in certain respects very much of its time. It was for one thing the time of the unheroic hero. Partly perhaps because of the Woman's Movement and a revulsion against Victorian empire-building, the heroic hero was suspect. Instead, sensitive, unaggressive young men like Rickie Elliot, Joyce's Stephen Dedalus and Lawrence's Paul Morel

---

[1] 'The Art of Fiction', interview of E. M. Forster by P. N. Furbank and F. J. H. Haskell in *Paris Review*, vol. 1 (Spring 1953).
[2] *Howards End*, chapter 6, p. 43. Abinger Edition, 1973.

were in fashion. In *The Longest Journey*, conventional heroism is ridiculed in the person of Gerald Dawes, Agnes's callow, arrogant fiancé, who is killed in a football match. Rickie's acerbic Aunt Emily declares that 'the chief characteristics of a hero are infinite disregard for the feelings of others, plus general inability to understand them'.[3] With protective irony, Joyce entitled the first version of his *Portrait*, *Stephen Hero*; and Strachey in *Eminent Victorians* demolished the culture heroes of the previous age.

Forster's distrust of heroes is openly expressed in his essay, 'What I Believe', written on the eve of the Second World War. 'They produce a desert of uniformity around them and often a pool of blood too, and I always feel a little man's pleasure when they come a cropper.' Instead he would prefer, he tells us, 'an aristocracy of the sensitive, the considerate and the plucky.'

If not always considerate or plucky, Forster's protagonists are at least sensitive. They are also easily muddled by the conflicting needs of their inner lives and the insistent demands of the outer as they struggle to achieve a selfhood that will accommodate inner need and outer fact. For them, as for many another protagonist in early modern fiction, self-discovery and self-realization are ultimate goals, a form of secular salvation, to be achieved, in the case of Forster's heroes, not by turning away from the world, like a monk or a mystic, but by embracing it. Philip is saved when he accepts Caroline's help and Gino's friendship. Mrs Moore is, in effect, damned when she rejects the world. The attempt to achieve a secular but nonetheless spiritual salvation is prominent in much of the literature contemporary with Forster's – in Conrad's and Lawrence's novels, for example, and in some of Shaw's plays.

In line with his emphasis on 'salvation', Forster, like other agnostic writers of the time, does not hesitate to apply religious, and specifically Christian language to secular situations. In addition to 'save' and 'salvation', his novels are well seasoned with words like 'holy', 'radiance', 'transfigure', and

---

[3] *The Longest Journey*, chapter 11, p. 121. New Directions, Norfolk, Conn.

'vision'. For Rickie the dell at Madingley is a 'kind of church', a 'holy place'. The pond in which George Emerson and his companions swim is significantly called The Sacred Lake; their swim is 'a passing benediction...a holiness, a spell, a momentary chalice for youth'. When Helen Schlegel and Paul Wilcox kiss under the wych-elm, the 'doors of heaven' are shaken open. Similarly, though in more strikingly ecclesiastical language, Joyce's Stephen conceives himself 'a priest of eternal imagination, transmuting the daily bread of experience into the radiant body of everlasting life'. James's Edwardian novels, as Richard Ellmann has observed, exhibit a fondness for words like 'save' and 'sacrifice'.[4] Mabel Pervin, in Lawrence's 'The Horse-Dealer's Daughter', gazes up at the man who has saved her from drowning with 'flaring, humble eyes of transfiguration'. Obviously, although these writers were professedly non-Christian, they felt a need to use Christian words in order to heighten spiritually significant episodes.

But Forster's use of religious words, like Joyce's and Lawrence's, is more than a matter of fashion. It conveys a fundamentally religious feeling for life – not for the next world but for the present one, not for God but for man. Wordly experience, Forster indicates, can even afford man a sense of transcendence, like that which a mystic gains through communion with God. Although God is permanent and life a flux, a moment lived with sufficient intensity can become, as it were, transcendent, seeming to stand, as Rickie Elliot puts it, for 'some eternal principle', against which lesser realities can be gauged. Rickie enjoys such moments in the dell at Madingley. Miss Raby experiences her one and crucial 'eternal moment' when she is kissed by the porter Feo during an outing in the Italian Alps. The elderly Mr Lucas has a transcedent experience in a grove of plane trees in Greece. Philip Herriton feels transported beyond himself in the opera house at Monteriano. And in a Marabar Cave, Mrs Moore has an inverted

---

[4] Richard Ellmann, 'Two Faces of Edward', in *Edwardians and Late Victorians*, English Institute Essays, 1959. My discussion of Forster's affinities with Joyce and other early modern writers is much indebted to Ellmann's essay.

eternal moment, an expression perhaps of Forster's own sense of ultimate nothingness. In this his last novel, eternity, instead of being vast and inspiring, a sign of essential and everlasting life, is confined within the claustral circumferance of a cave that echoingly reverberates the visitor's doubts and fantasies.

Forster's 'eternal moments' have roots in nineteenth-century literature as well as in universal mystical experience. Wordsworth saw the most memorable events in his childhood as so many 'spots of time', the 'types and symbols of eternity'. Shelley, Browning, Rossetti, and other poets stressed the timelessness of intense and privileged moments; and Pater declared it a purpose of art to convey, through the depiction of such moments, a sense of eternity. Writers contemporary with Forster continued to find in fleeting moments a heightened and timeless reality. Joyce calls them epiphanies – sudden manifestations of essential life, of which Stephen's experiences are crucial to his development. For Lawrence they are 'baptisms of fire', periods when the 'dark gods' of the buried self are revitalized. That passing moments can be endowed with timeless meaning is a belief underlying much of Virginia Woolf's fiction and Proust's.[5]

In seeking to arrest and transcendentalize such moments, all of these writers, both nineteenth and twentieth century, were, in effect, trying to endow private experience with quasi-religious value. For if, as much of the philosophy of the eighteenth and nineteenth century indicates, the world that we perceive is not the world in itself but only our private experience of it, then we can never really transcend ourselves and sense the divine. Religious truth becomes subjective; and, consequently, intense and privileged moments can attain a heightened value. When Mrs Moore discovers that all her divine insights are confined to the cave of her own mind, she becomes deranged. Her God and her eternity, it would seem, are not 'up there'; they are within her cave.

[5] For an excellent discussion of the treatment of time in nineteenth- and early-twentieth-century literature, see Jerome Buckley, *The Triumph of Time* (especially chapter 8). Harvard University Press, 1966.

Forster's religious feeling for life embraces the unseen –
that irrational and unpredictable force in man and nature that
often subverts man's attempts to impose order upon his surroundings. The equivalent of Lawrence's 'dark gods', the
unseen is potentially liberating and destructive, and perhaps
partly expresses Forster's apprehensions about being homosexual. The young Maurice's developing homosexuality is one
sign of the unseen; the echo that breaks loose in the Marabar
Caves, another. Who can say if these manifestations are good
or evil, constructive or destructive? In their ultimate reach they
are both.

Forster's sense of the unseen and a susceptibility to literary
fashion underlie his fictional use of myth and fantasy.[6] Pan
appears in 'The Story of a Panic', a faun in 'The Curate's
Friend'. 'Other Kingdom' is based on the legend of Daphne
and Apollo. Such stories may strike the modern reader as
precious and artificial; and that is the way they evidently struck
Forster's Bloomsbury friends. '"The Point of It",' Forster has
said, 'was ill-liked by my Bloomsbury friends when it came out.
"What *is* the point of it?" they queried thinly, nor did I know
what to reply.'[7] According to David Garnett, such friends as
Leonard and Virginia Woolf, Clive Bell and Roger Fry may
have exercised a restraining influence on Forster's fictional use
of myth and fantasy.[8]

Whether or not this was the case, myth and fantasy play an
occasional, though usually more muted role in the novels and
later short stories. Rickie, like his creator, writes mythological
tales. The wych-elm at Howards End, with a row of pig's teeth
stuck in it, has a mythical force. And the Marabar Caves
show Forster's ability to create myth and give it psychological
relevance. Several of Forster's characters – for example, Mr
Emerson, Mrs Wilcox, Miss Avery and, most successfully, Mrs
Moore – are quasi-mythological. They are in tune with the

[6] See Patricia Merivale, *Pan the Goat-God, his Myth in Modern Times*. Harvard
University Press, 1969.
[7] See Forster's Introduction to *Collected Tales*. New York, 1952.
[8] David Garnett, 'Forster and Bloomsbury' in *Aspects of E. M. Forster*, ed.
Oliver Stallybrass. New York, 1969.

unseen and lead others to recognize its role in their lives. Of the seven posthumously published short stories written after 1926, three – 'Dr Woolacott', 'The Classical Annex' and 'The Torque' – contain some element of fantasy. Thus Forster's recurrent use of myth and fantasy throughout his career testifies to his sustained sense of the unseen. There is more to life, he suggests, than the prevailing materialism of our age can account for.

II

'I am quite sure I am not a great novelist,' Forster told an interviewer in 1959;[9] and probably few readers would wish to dispute this claim. Well as he manages many of his effects, his range and sympathies are too narrow to class him among the Tolstoys, Dostoevskys and Prousts. His most vital characters are, generally speaking, those to whom in real life he would have probably been attracted – a varied group, to be sure, although all of them are sensitive to the needs of their inner lives. Most of them belong to the English upper-middle-class – people with enough money and leisure to travel and cultivate their interests. Of those who fall outside this class, all are male and non-English: Gino, Aziz, Godbole, and perhaps Cocoanut, the half-caste native in 'The Other Boat'.

Into several of his important characters, Forster clearly fails to breathe life, or enough life. Stephen Wonham, George Emerson, Henry Wilcox and Alec Scudder are comparative failures. And they fail perhaps because Forster was too intent upon fixing them with certain moral and spiritual qualities rather than allowing them to grow organically. That is to say, he envisioned the qualities first, then invented the characters to fit them, and the results are thin and wooden.

Forster's treatment of heterosexual love – for reasons now clear – is equally unconvincing. One need only contrast the pallid, manipulated connection between Margaret Schlegel and Henry Wilcox, or Adela Quested's equally dry engage-

[9] An interview with Monica Campbell on the occasion of Forster's eightieth birthday. B.B.C.

ment to Ronny Heaslop, with Maurice's passion for Clive Durham or Lionel March's for Cocoanut, to test the validity of this judgment.

In his early novels, and also in *Maurice*, Forster, sometimes identifying himself with his main character, writes in an inflatedly emotional style. A notable instance of such sentimentality is the scene in *The Longest Journey* in which Agnes and Gerald kiss and Rickie, watching them, feels himself standing 'at the springs of creation', hearing 'the primeval monotony', and a great deal more besides.[10] As indicated in chapter 6 above, *Maurice* is also weakened by Forster's too obvious empathy with his eponymous hero.

But the limitations and weaknesses of Forster's fiction are minor when set against its virtues. And it is because of its virtues that his best fiction is still enjoyed.

For one thing, it is morally realistic. In Forster's fictional world, as in the real one, individual actions, however well intentioned, have unpredictable consequences. The Schlegels' kindness to Leonard Bast prepares the way for his murder. The excursion to the Marabar Caves that Aziz arranges in order to entertain his English friends precipitates the death of one of them and dislocates an entire community. As Lionel Trilling long ago pointed out, Forster's novels reveal a network of moral forces in which everybody is implicated.[11] In today's impersonal world, in which it is always tempting to blame 'the others' for overpopulation, pollution and most of our other problems, Forster's moral realism is provocative and refreshing.

Forster's fiction is also rich in psychological insight. Consider the realism and sensitivity with which Forster develops Maurice's passion for Clive. Or the following passage in which Aziz, looking at a photograph of his wife, tries to recollect her:

And unlocking a drawer, he took out his wife's photograph. He gazed at it, and tears spouted from his eyes. He thought, 'How unhappy I am!' But because he really was unhappy, another emotion soon mingled with his self-pity: he desired to remember his wife and could not. Why could he

---

[10] *The Longest Journey*, chapter 3, p. 52. New Directions, Norfolk, Conn.
[11] Lionel Trilling, *E. M. Forster*, chapter 1. Norfolk, Conn., 1943.

remember people whom he did not love? They were always so vivid to him, whereas the more he looked at this photograph, the less he saw. She had eluded him thus, ever since they had carried her to her tomb. He had known that she would pass from his hands and eyes, but had thought she could live in his mind, not realizing that the very fact that we have loved the dead increases their unreality, and that the more passionately we invoke them the further they recede. A piece of brown cardboard and three children – that was all that was left of his wife. It was unbearable, and he thought again, 'How unhappy I am!' and became happier. He had breathed for an instant the mortal air that surrounds Orientals and all men, and he drew back from it with a gasp, for he was young.[12]

A lesser novelist would have sentimentalized such a scene, presenting not a living heart and mind but a series of emotional clichés.

Forster's psychological realism is reflected in his dialogue, which often conveys the voice and mind of the speakers, as, for example, in the meeting between Mrs Moore and Aziz outside the mosque:

'Madam! Madam! Madam!'
  'Oh! Oh!' the woman gasped.
  'Madam, this is a mosque, you have no right here at all; you should have taken off your shoes; this is a holy place for Moslems.'
  'I have taken them off.'
  'You have?'
  'I left them at the entrance.'
  'Then I ask your pardon.'
  Still startled, the woman moved out, keeping the ablution-tank between them. He called after her, 'I am truly sorry for speaking.'
  'Yes, I was right, was I not? If I remove my shoes, I am allowed?'
  'Of course, but so few ladies take the trouble, especially if thinking no one is there to see.'
  'That makes no difference. God is here.'
  'Madam!'
  'Please let me go.'
  'Oh, can I do you some service now or at any time?'
  'No, thank you, really none – good night.'
  'May I know your name?'
  She was now in the shadow of the gateway, so that he could not see her face, but she saw his, and she said with a change of voice, 'Mrs Moore'.

There is some good dialogue, too, when Lionel March, having just escaped from a nighttime quarrel with Cocoanut in their

[12] *A Passage to India*, chapter 6, pp. 56–7. Harcourt, Brace, New York, 1952.

cabin, unexpectedly meets Colonel Arbuthnot on the ship's main deck:

'Hullo, who's that, what's there?'
　'March, sir, Lionel March. I'm afraid I've disturbed you.'
　'No, no, Lionel, that's all right, I wasn't asleep. Ye gods, what gorgeous pyjamas the fellow's wearing. What's he going about like a lone wolf for? Eh?'
　'Too hot in my cabin, sir, Nothing sinister.'
　'How goes the resident wog?'
　'The resident wog he sleeps.'
　'By the way, what's his name?'
　'Moraes, I believe.'

Forster has a striking gift for comedy and satire. His comedy is social, his satire light but penetrating. The dramatic and ironic development of such scenes as the trip to Fiesole in *A Room with a View* and Fielding's tea-party in *A Passage to India* recall Jane Austen. But Forster's range is wider than hers, not simply because it embraces foreigners and foreign settings, but because it is often infused with a sense of infinity and the unseen, as when Godbole ends the tea-party with his 'song of the unknown bird'. 'Ronny's steps had died away, and there was a moment of absolute silence. No ripple disturbed the water, no leaf stirred.'

Like Dickens, Forster can enliven a comic portrait with a few deft touches. One recalls Miss Bartlett 'talking to Mr Beebe, and as she spoke, her long narrow head drove backwards and forwards, slowly, regularly, as though she were demolishing some invisible obstacle'. On Herbert Pembroke, who, 'though not in orders...had the air of being on the verge of them'. Or Mrs Turton, who 'was "saving herself up," as she called it – not for anything that would happen that afternoon or even that week, but for some vague future occasion when a high official might come along and tax her social strength. Most of her public appearances were marked by this air of reserve.'

Forster's sense of humour and comedy distinguish him from Lawrence, a novelist whose vision of modern life has much in common with his. Unlike Forster, however, who was temperamentally sceptical, Lawrence had faith and a sense of mission. He believed that man could be saved if only he could recover his buried self, stifled by modern life; and he wrote with a prophetic fervour in order to save him. At his best he wrote with a passion and poetry beyond Forster's range. But not surprisingly he lacks humour. Prophets and saviours usually do.

A final word must be said about Forster's personal voice, which marks every page of his fiction. It is the voice of a humanist – one seriously committed to human values while refusing to take himself too seriously. Its tone is inquiring, not dogmatic. It reflects a mind aware of the complexities confronting those who wish to live spiritually satisfying, morally responsible lives in a world that increasingly militates against the individual's needs. Sensitively and often profoundly, Forster's fiction explores the problems such people encounter. And for this reason it is emphatically a fiction for our time.